00017283

G000295882

G000295882

1 2 7 • 5   N A T H

E V I D E N C E   A N D   A S S U R

WITHDRAWN FROM STOCK
U.C.C. LIBRARY

AN LEABHARLANN
COLÁISTE NA hOLLSCOILE, CORCAIGH

Níl sé ceaduithe an leabhar seo a choimead thar an dáta is déanaí
atá luaite thíos.
This book must be returned not later than the last date stamped
below.

19 JAN 1987

The Library, University College, Cork

WITHDRAWN FROM STOCK
U.C.C. LIBRARY

CAMBRIDGE STUDIES IN PHILOSOPHY

Evidence and assurance

CAMBRIDGE STUDIES IN PHILOSOPHY

General editor D. H. MELLOR

Advisory editors J. E. J. ALTHAM, SIMON BLACKBURN, DANIEL DENNETT, MARTIN HOLLIS, FRANK JACKSON, T. J. SMILEY, BARRY STROUD

JAMES CARGILE *Paradoxes: a study in form and predication*
PAUL M. CHURCHLAND *Scientific realism and the plasticity of mind*
N. M. L. NATHAN *Evidence and assurance*

121. 5 NATH
172831

Evidence and assurance

N. M. L. Nathan

Senior Lecturer in Philosophy
University of East Anglia

Cambridge University Press

CAMBRIDGE

LONDON NEW YORK NEW ROCHELLE

MELBOURNE SYDNEY

Published by the Press Syndicate of the University of Cambridge
The Pitt Building, Trumpington Street, Cambridge CB2 1RP
32 East 57th Street, New York, NY 10022, USA
296 Beaconsfield Parade, Middle Park, Melbourne 3206, Australia

© Cambridge University Press 1980

First published 1980

Set, printed and bound in Great Britain by
Fakenham Press Limited, Fakenham, Norfolk

Library of Congress Cataloguing in Publication Data
Nathan, N M L
Evidence and assurance.
(Cambridge studies in philosophy)
Bibliography: p.
Includes index.
1. Evidence. 2. Justification (Theory of knowledge)
3. Belief and doubt. 4. Skepticism. I. Title.
II. Series.
BC173.N37   121   79–50505
ISBN 0 521 22517 5

Contents

Acknowledgments

My thanks are due to the Alexander von Humboldt-Stiftung, for providing me with time to work on this book, and to Professor Wolfgang Stegmüller, for access to his seminar in the University of Munich. I would also like to thank Professor R. G. Swinburne, Professor G. H. Bird and Dr J. E. J. Altham for comments on previous versions, and Professor S. Körner for some early encouragement. Parts of Chapter 4 have appeared in D. Papenfuss and W. Söring (eds.), *Transzendenz und Immanenz*, and are reprinted by permission of Kohlhammer Verlag, Stuttgart.

N.M.L.N.

University of East Anglia
Norwich

Introduction

Scepticism is the doctrine that little or nothing is known or rationally believed or the object of justified belief. And a boring enough doctrine it is, unless the sceptic can somehow show that his sense of 'knowledge', 'rationality' or 'justification' is our sense also, or would be our sense if there were more of the truth in what we believed. Really to disturb us, he must reveal something which would make us go on hopelessly wanting to apply his cognitive concepts no matter what we were reminded of by the most faithful delineation of common sense. It is his failure to engage in this way with our actual or potential desires, the privacy and arbitrariness of his claims about what knowledge or rationality essentially is, that makes us tire so quickly with the sceptic as currently portrayed in the epistemological handbooks. The knowledge we have so little of turns out to be knowledge merely of propositions whose truth follows logically from the fact that they are believed, or knowledge of necessary truths, or absolute certainty. Easily persuaded of the artificiality of these standards, we turn away, grateful for the reminder of how different mathematics is from empirical science.

There is however a quite different sceptical doctrine, not obviously dependent on the inapplicability of some artificially demanding cognitive concept, and towards which anyone who has tried to disentangle recent debates on foundations and coherence theories of justification must have felt at least some passing attraction. It is that for much of what we believe an infinite regress of justification is both necessary and impossible. May it not be that we do actually want a justified belief impossible to possess unless justificatory regression can somehow be brought to a stop? Are we not perhaps also liable on reflection to want a justified belief which, though not requiring absolute certainty or incorrigibility in the stopping-place, does nevertheless require a non-arbitrary terminus hardly ever possible to reach? In what follows I try to articulate a version of this regressive sceptical doctrine, and to support it with the strongest arguments I am able to construct.

'Radical assurance' will be my label for the species of justified believing power to gain which we are I think liable so often to want in vain. Three logically necessary conditions for being radically assured of the truth of a proposition are that you have assured yourself of its truth by a conscious and deliberate activity of investigation, that you are aware of the nature of this investigation, and that the proposition in question is actually true. One method of gaining assurance of a proposition's truth would be consciously to affirm that some other particular proposition is evidence for its truth, and consciously to affirm that other proposition itself. Your assurance would then be evidential. Another method might be somehow simply to investigate the proposition's own content without considering whether any other proposition is evidence for its truth. Your assurance would then be intuitive. But however your assurance is reached it will not be radical unless you reach it by a deliberate activity of investigation and have a certain insight into the nature of that activity. Additionally, radical assurance is in a certain sense regressive. It is logically necessary that if you are radically and evidentially assured that p, then you are also radically assured not only of the truth of the further proposition that you believe to be evidence for p, but also of the proposition that this further proposition *is* evidence for p.

My first thesis is that the scope of radical assurance is very severely limited by these various necessary conditions. From their conjunction with certain plausible psychological contingencies, it follows that you are radically assured that p only if one or other of the following three further conditions is satisfied. (1) p is self-evident, i.e. true and such that its truth can be in a certain sense metaphorically seen. (2) p is in a certain way evidentially related to a self-evident proposition. (3) An infinite regress of assurance is possible. But no such regress is possible, and even if there were propositions whose truth was seeable in the requisite metaphorical sense, there would not be enough of them for the other two conditions to be very often satisfied.

My second thesis is that although radical assurance is not something you actually aim for in ordinary daily or even scientific investigations, you are nevertheless liable, in other circumstances, to want much more radical assurance, or much more extensive powers to gain it, than you can ever actually possess. You are liable, when reflecting about your belief-system as a whole, to want radical assurance of the truth of all those propositions you believe whose truth-value you do not find a matter of indifference. And you are liable, when reflecting on the traditional problem of the sources of knowledge, to want the power to be radically assured of the truth of many of the kinds of propositions which outer-sensory experience has non-radically assured you of. The point here is not that sensory assurance leaves genuine doubts about 'the external world' which only radical assurance is powerful enough to remove, but that you are not sure that the power to gain that radical assurance would not be an inevitable concomitant of the power to resolve quite other and more genuine doubts about what precise varieties of knowledge-yielding experience we actually enjoy.

Thirdly, there is the question of consolation. Scepticism about radical assurance is, as I said, not just another altar to the incorrigible, not something you can be deflected from by the simple reminder of how much lower our ordinary standards really are. Necessarily, *p* is true if you are radically assured that *p*. But you can be radically assured that *p* without *p*'s following from the proposition that you believe *p*, and radically and evidentially assured that *p* is true without having conclusive evidence for its truth. *p* may also itself be a proposition to the effect that some other proposition is no more than probably true. Nor do I see any reason to suppose that the desire for radical assurance which philosophical reflection is liable to generate or reveal will vanish completely on the further realisation that it can hardly ever be satisfied. It is however worth asking whether we can assure ourselves that things would really have been better if our power to gain radical assurance had been less limited. We cannot be *radically* assured that things would have been no better, or not at any rate unless the scope of self-evidence is very much broader than most people are seriously prepared to believe. But I will show that if you are lucky enough to have certain other beliefs, then even on modest assumptions about the scope of self-evidence, your belief that things would have been no better can as it happens be an assurance almost as satisfactory as the radical kind. And if you are not lucky in this way, certain further more or less recondite crumbs of consolation may still remain.

Chapter 1 is about the nature of radical assurance. Chapter 2 explains the restrictions on its scope. My arguments about our liability to want radical assurance or the power to get it come in Chapter 3. In Chapter 4 I relate my scepticism to current doctrines about how to terminate or circumvent an infinite regress of justification. Chapter 5 is about arguments to the effect that many contingent propositions must be in some sense knowable or capable of justified acceptance if any sentence is meaningful, or any proposition believed. I try to make sure that such arguments cannot be adapted to show that my assumptions about the restricted scope of radical assurance are exaggerated or unintelligible. In Chapters 6 and 7 I look at the relations between scepticism about radical assurance and some familiar and ostensibly more limited forms of scepticism about ethics and induction. Chapter 8 is on the question of consolation.

But before beginning in earnest, and confronting you with the rather complex apparatus on which my subsequent arguments depend, there are one or two possible misunderstandings worth trying to anticipate.

In the first place, pessimism about the scope of radical assurance will probably not entail pessimism about the scope of knowledge. It may very well be that some knowing amounts to no more than a causal relation between the believer and the object of his belief and requires no conscious activity of investigation or inference on the believer's part. In this case there can be knowledge without any kind of assurance, radical or otherwise. But if I am right in thinking that an extensive power to gain radical assurance is something we are anyway liable to want, then doubts about whether this is something we can ever possess will not be any the less disturbing for their failure to entail corresponding doubts about our power to know. Causal theories of knowledge do not abolish volitional and regressive difficulties – they merely transfer them to a different department of philosophy.

I said that what limits our power to gain radical assurance is that when p is not self-evident we cannot be radically assured of its truth unless a regress of assurance is terminable in the believing of a self-evident proposition which is evidentially related to p. Surely this is to embrace the implausibilities of a *foundations* theory of justification? Why have I not grasped that whether a man is justified in believing a proposition depends on the *coherence* of this proposition with the other propositions which he believes? I shall argue, in Chapter 4, that this objection rests on a failure to distinguish between the conditions under which a man can assure himself that a proposition is true, and the conditions under which one proposition is evidence for another proposition, where '*q* is evidence for *p*' means, on the roughest possible preliminary approximation, that when a proposition like *q* is true so usually at least is a proposition like *p*. I do not deny that there are concepts of coherence such that if *q* is a proposition to the effect that *p* belongs to a coherent set of propositions, then *q* is evidence for *p*. But if a man aims to *assure* himself that *p* is true by affirming as evidence a proposition about *p*'s membership of a coherent set, then the question arises of whether he will not also want to assure himself that this proposition about *p*'s set-membership is true. And if he affirms some further proposition as evidence for the proposition about *p*'s set-membership he may also want to assure himself in turn that this further proposition is true. An infinite regress threatens, and no theory concerned only with evidential relations between propositions will show us how to avoid it. 'Foundations theory of assurance' would be a useful enough name for the view, which I accept, that the regress must be terminable if we are to have the sort of assurance we are liable to want or liable to want the power to gain. But there would be no incompatibility, on that definition, between a foundations theory of assurance and a coherence theory of evidence. Confusion arises because of the multiplicity of uses to which 'justification' and its cognates are currently put. We talk of one proposition's justifying another, meaning that the first proposition supports or is evidence for the second. We talk also of a man's being justified in believing a proposition. This may mean merely that he has that right or entitlement to believe a proposition which derives from its being at least probably true, or alternatively that right to believe it which derives from the fact that his believing it would be by some decision-theoretic standard better than not believing it. But it may also mean something which entails that he has deliberately *done* something to assure himself that the proposition is true or that his believing it meets the decision-theoretic standard. The terminology of 'justified belief' is as chaotic as the terminology of 'rational belief' and 'rational action'.

But now, given that we must at any rate terminate a regress of assurance, why exactly should it be supposed that this is something we are so rarely able to do? And what in particular of the familiar stopping-places of foundational epistemology – beliefs justified by

sense-experience, self-justifying beliefs, beliefs for which justification is simply not needed? The first two options are eliminated, as I
will argue, if justified belief is taken to be an assurance of truth
gained through a deliberate and self-conscious activity of investigation. For consciousness of the nature of one's sensory assurance
transmutes it into an affirmation of evidence. And it cannot follow
logically from the fact that you believe something that you have
conducted an active investigation into its truth-value. The 'no-
need' theory is stricken by a different ambiguity: can we ask 'Not
needed for what?', or does 'not needed' mean simply 'not good
actually to have'?

Another likely objection is that scepticism about radical assurance
defeats itself. I have already promised to answer one version of this
charge, namely that it is a condition for the meaningfulness of any
sentence or for any proposition to be believed that radical assurance
has more scope than I am prepared to assume. But there is another
way in which my contentions could seem self-defeating. If there are
no self-evident propositions, or too few of them for us to have a
power of radical assurance as extensive as we are liable to want, then
how can there be enough self-evident propositions for me radically
to assure myself that even my own sceptical theses are true? How
can I be radically assured that we really are liable to want a belief-
system in which every proposition believed is one of whose truth
we have radical assurance? How can I be radically assured that the
impossibility of an infinite regress of assurance makes radical assurance dependent on the scope of self-evidence, or even that the scope
of self-evidence is as limited as I say it is?

But I do not advance these theses about radical assurance because
I believe that I can radically assure myself of their truth. I advance
them because I believe them, want you to believe them, and believe
that you will believe them if you follow my arguments. Since you
are liable to believe that some though not many propositions are
self-evident, it is worth trying to show that, on what I take to be
typically modest assumptions about the scope of self-evidence, it is
possible radically to assure oneself that some of my theses are true,
and in particular that we can be radically assured of the impossibility
of an infinite regress of evidential assurance. But I do not claim that
modest assumptions about the scope of self-evidence would allow
us to be radically assured that these same assumptions are ever
actually made, or that radical assurance is something we are liable to

want. Nor do I claim that we can be radically assured of the truth of any proposition to the effect that some particular proposition categorically is or is not self-evident or one of whose truth we can be radically assured. It is not even essential to my position that there actually *are* any self-evident propositions. If there were none at all, then my theses about radical assurance could still be true. They would then all be in the same position that only some of them would be in if typically modest assumptions about the scope of self-evidence were true.

Finally, the talk of consolation may have struck you as a trifle theatrical. Surely the answer lies simply in the unavoidable self-assertion of nature and common sense? No one can actually succeed in living like Pyrrho, in the absurd description of Montaigne: 'dull and impassive, adopting a surly and unsociable way of life, getting in the way of jostling carts, defying precipices, refusing to obey the laws'. There are forms of scepticism to which this objection does apply, but they do not include scepticism about radical assurance. To deny that you can be radically assured that *p* is not to deny *p*, or even to claim that not believing *p* is a psychological possibility. I nowhere encourage the 'Cartesian' thought of a man contracting the body of what he believes until it coincides with what he can immediately validate and then trying desperately to expand it again, according to the rule that nothing should be accepted which is not self-evidently derivable from that basis. It is not common-sense propositions about chairs and tables and precipices that we are not to believe, but optimistic philosophical propositions about the attainability of our potential cognitive desires. 'La raison confond les dogmatiques, et la nature confond les pyrrhoniens.'

I

The nature of radical assurance

Radical assurance lies somewhere in the wild medley of things you might talk of in saying that a belief is rational or justified. And one relatively easy step towards its location is to mark off a form of rationally believing *p* whose rationality is contingent upon your also believing certain propositions about the relations between the values of the possible outcomes of your believing *p* and the values of the possible outcomes of your not believing *p*. It helps to contrast rational belief of this kind – I will call it consequentially rational belief – with the generic assurance of which radical assurance is one particular species. You assure yourself that *p*, on my stipulation at any rate, only if you satisfy yourself of its truth by a conscious and deliberate investigation of its truth-value. And that you have assured yourself that *p* neither entails nor is entailed by the proposition that you are consequentially rational in believing *p*. I will say something about consequentially rational belief and its relations with assurance of truth in section (1) of this chapter. And there will be more details about assurance itself in section (2). After distinguishing there between evidential and experiential modes of assurance and dealing in some detail with the experiential mode, I move on in section (3) to a correspondingly detailed discussion of the evidential mode. By section (4) I am able finally to define radical assurance, and to contrast it with knowledge and the chaos of 'justified belief'. The preliminaries are completed in section (5) which contains more about radical assurance of the non-evidential kind.

(1) *Consequentially rational belief*

The old man is in no position actually to find out whether or not his housekeeper is honest but he does think that in his present precarious emotional state, it will be dangerous for everyone if he believes that she is not, or even if he does not believe that she is. This makes it consequentially rational for him to believe that she is honest. You are consequentially rational in believing p if you believe a certain proposition about the relations between the values of the possible outcomes of your believing p and values of the possible outcomes of your not believing p. And this proposition about outcomes is the proposition you must believe in order to be rational in the action of getting yourself to believe p. If it is consequentially rational for the old man to believe that his housekeeper is honest, then it is rational for him to do what he can to make himself believe that she is. And that course of action is rational because of what he believes about the outcomes of his believing and not believing her honest.

In ordinary usage, a rational action can be either an action for which the agent believes that there is a reason, or an action for which the agent believes correctly that there is a reason, or an action for which there is a reason, even though the agent does not believe that there is. We could mark the distinctions by talking of subjectively, objectively and unconsciously rational action. For the purpose of defining consequentially rational belief, I neglect unconsciously rational action, and assume that it is a necessary condition for you to be rational in doing something that you believe that there is a reason to do it. But we can if we like distinguish between subjective and objective modes of consequentially rational belief. The old man's belief that his housekeeper is honest will be consequentially rational in the objective mode only if he was right about how dangerous it would have been for him not to have believed this, only if he was correct in thinking that there was a reason for him to get himself to believe that she was honest. And his belief will be consequentially rational in the subjective mode if his calculation, though deliberate and explicit, was nevertheless based on a mistake: there was nothing very precarious about his emotional state, no danger in his not believing that she was honest.

But now, undercutting these niceties, you will probably object that there is something paradoxical about applying *any* notion of rationality to the enterprise of deliberately setting out to end up with a belief. Suppose that a man, believing his son dead, decides in his misery to be hypnotised into believing that the boy is still alive. An objection to this kind of project, according to Bernard Williams, is that there is no end to the amount you have to pull down. It is like a revolutionary movement trying to extirpate the last remains of the *ancien régime*. The man gets rid of this belief about his son, and then there is some belief which strongly implies that his son is dead, and that has to be got rid of. Then there is another belief which could lead his thoughts in the undesired direction, and that has to be got rid of. It might be that a project of this kind tended in the end to involve total destruction of the world of reality.[1]

We might of course reply that the danger of being involved in an endless extirpation of evidence is precisely one of those possible outcomes of believing *p* which the consequentially rational man should consider in deciding whether or not it is better to do what results in his believing *p*. But apart from that, and more importantly, there is a distinction between setting out to believe something, and setting out to believe what you already know to be false. It does not follow from your being consequentially rational in believing *p*, as I defined it, that you antecedently knew that *p* was false; nor indeed does it follow that *p* is the sort of proposition which you ever will or even could have convincing evidence either for or against.

Williams does however have a further doubt. He presents this as a reason for its not being a contingent fact that I cannot bring it about, just like that, that I believe something, as it is a contingent fact 'that I cannot bring it about, just like that, that I'm blushing'. But if what he says here is true, it will I think also show that there is something paradoxical even in more roundabout methods of deliberately getting yourself to end up with a belief.

If in full consciousness I could will to acquire a 'belief' irrespective of its truth, it is unclear that before the event I could seriously think of it as a belief, i.e. as something purporting to represent reality. At the very least, there must be a restriction on what is the case after the event; since I could not then, in full consciousness, regard this as a belief of mine, i.e. something I take to be true, and also know that I acquired it at will . . . But if I can acquire beliefs at will I must know that I am able to do this: and how could I know that I was capable of this feat, if with regard to every feat of this kind which I had performed I necessarily had to believe that it had not taken place?[2]

[1] Williams (1973) p. 151
[2] Williams (1973) p. 148

You might as well say that you cannot sincerely believe something and at the same time recognise that it was the fashionableness of its opposite that originally made you believe it. There is no problem here if you also think that, luckily enough, fashion was in this case wrong. And of course, given that you really were as counter-suggestible as you now think, and do now actually *believe* whatever it is that it was once so fashionable to reject, you will be inconsistent if you do *not* think that fashion was in this case wrong. In the same way, if, having actually *succeeded* in willing yourself to acquire some belief, you now believe that this is how you acquired it, you are bound to believe that as luck would have it it is a true belief that you willed yourself to acquire. This being so, there is no reason why you should not also know that you willed yourself to acquire it.

Another writer suggests, less comprehensibly, that because believing a proposition is not much like doing something, we cannot 'properly' talk of there being a reason for believing a proposition *p* except in a sense which implies that some other proposition is evidence for *p*'s truth. That it would make things easier for his relatives if he believed that he was cured is a reason 'for doing something of a description in which the belief figures; it is not a reason for believing that he is cured'.[1] This is because 'if in being or doing *x*, *A* thereby does *y*, the fact that *A* thereby does *y* can be a reason that *A* can have for being or doing *x* only if it is possible for *A* to be or do *x* intentionally, and to intend to be or do *x* in order to do *y*'.[2] But if being *x* intentionally in order to do *y* is possible at all, as it surely is, then I do not see why the man cannot intentionally believe that he is cured in order to make things easier for his relatives. To say that she is intentionally shabby-looking in order to convince people that she is above all frivolity and a totally committed Party member is to imply that she has done things which, as she intended, result in her looking shabby, and done them because she thought she would thereby convince people of how deeply committed she was to the Party. Why cannot a man likewise do things which, as he intended, result in his believing that he is cured, and do them because he thinks that his believing that he is cured would make things easier for his relatives? As I will argue in a moment, consequentially rational belief is in a way dependent on investigations aimed solely at discovering the truth: there is always some proposition whose actual truth you must

---

[1] Edgley (1969) p. 63
[2] ibid. p. 61

be assured of if you are to avoid all arbitrariness in your consequentially rational belief. But it is I think wrong to suppose that there is anything irresolubly paradoxical in consequentially rational belief as such.

But before coming on to the relations between consequentially rational belief and assurance of truth, I must say a little more about the different modes of consequentially rational belief itself. Since being consequentially rational in believing *p* is a matter of being rational in action designed to result in your believing *p*, there are as many different modes of consequentially rational belief as there are modes of rational action. We have already exploited the distinction between believing, and believing correctly, that there is a reason for action. That gave us subjective and objective modes of rational belief. Decision-theoretic classifications of rational action are another obvious resource.

Suppose you are engaged in a 'game against nature' in conditions of uncertainty: you must decide between alternative actions whose outcomes are determined by chance rather than the calculated decisions of some other agent or agents, and decide without the help of any beliefs about the probabilities of the possible outcomes. I might tell you to perform that action whose worst outcome is at least as good as the best outcome of any of the other actions you think available, and whose best outcome is better than the best outcome of any of the other actions you think available (dominance rule). Or to perform that action whose worst possible outcome is better than the worst possible outcome of any of the other actions you think available (maximin rule). Or to suppose for purposes of calculation that all possible outcomes are equiprobable and then perform that action with the highest expected value, where the expected value of an action is calculated by multiplying the probability of each possible outcome of the action by the value of that outcome, and then adding together the products (Laplacean rule). And so on.[1] To each rule there corresponds a mode of rational action which requires the agent to believe that his action satisfies that rule. And to each such decision-theoretically distinguished mode of rational action there corresponds a mode of consequentially rational belief. You will be consequentially rational in believing *p* in the dominance mode only if you antecedently believed that the worst outcome of your believing *p* is at least as good as the best outcome

[1] See Luce and Raiffa (1957) Ch. 13

of your not believing *p* and that the best outcome of your believing *p* is better than the best outcome of your not believing *p*. And so on.

Pascal's fragment 'Infini-rien'[1] illustrates several of the different modes of consequentially rational belief which I have distinguished so far.[2] Suppose that nothing could be better than the outcome of believing that the Catholic God exists when this proposition is true, that nothing could be worse than the outcome of not believing this proposition when it is true, and that the outcome of believing it when it is false is neither better nor worse than the outcome of not believing it when it is false. There are then no circumstances in which not believing that the Catholic God exists has a better outcome than believing it, and one circumstance in which believing it has a better outcome than not believing it has in any circumstances. Suppose you believe all these propositions about the value of outcomes and decide in consequence to do what will result in your believing that the Catholic God exists (to 'take holy water, have masses said, etc.'). Your believing that the Catholic God exists is then consequentially rational in the dominance mode. Or maybe you think that if the Catholic God does not exist, there is more happpiness in not believing that he does than in believing that he does. Pascal has a separate argument from that assumption, and it illustrates consequentially rational believing in the Laplacean mode. We are to suppose that you do not believe that there is any good evidence either for or against the existence of the Catholic God and that you do what will result in that believing which has the highest expected value on the assumption that his existence and his non-existence are equiprobable. You will be consequentially rational in believing that the God exists because half of what could not be better plus half of what could be very much worse must add up to something more valuable than half of what could not be worse plus half of what could be a great deal better. Lastly, a man might want to maximise expected value without assuming that the existence and non-existence of the Catholic God are precisely equiprobable. The infinite benefit of believing that the God exists when this is true, and the infinite loss of not believing it when it is true conspire to guarantee the same result as before, for any probability greater than zero which he ascribes to the God's existence. There are many ways of arguing that even in these last two cases the consequentially rational

---

[1] *Pensées* (Pléiade ed.) No. 451
[2] I rely here on Hacking's illuminating commentary (1972)

believing is merely subjective. Consequentially rational believing is objective only if you believe true propositions about the value of possible outcomes. The non-existence of the Catholic God is logically compatible with the existence of a jehovah who damns all who toy with holy water and sacraments, and so with the possibility that nothing could be worse than believing in the Catholic God when he does not exist.

Another obvious distinction would be between global and local modes of consequentially rational belief. The global mode would require you to have evaluated the outcomes of your believing and not believing the proposition in question in the light of *all* your general beliefs about what kinds of things are valuable. For the local mode it would be necessary and sufficient that you had taken only some of these general beliefs into account. The consequentially rational believing in Pascal's examples may or may not be in the global mode, or may not involve more than a purely prudential evaluation of possible outcomes.[1] But there is a clear example of a merely local mode of consequentially rational believing in scientific investigation as conceived of by some recent theorists of 'epistemic utility'. The scientist, according to Levi, believes scientific hypotheses as opposed to propositions to the effect that such and such a scientific hypothesis is more or less probable, and he is to evaluate these believings by considering the values and probabilities of the various possible outcomes of believing and not believing the scientific hypotheses in question. But in evaluating these outcomes he is to consider nothing other than the supposed intrinsic value of believing the truth, believing something ('relieving agnosticism'), believing something simple and believing something with explanatory power.[2] He may not for example consider the political capital to be made out of the fact that someone of his authority believes something with such depressing implications for the future of parliamentary democracy.

I have now said enough about consequentially rational belief to contrast it in a rather more specific way with assurance of truth. You assure yourself that *p*, I said, only if you satisfy yourself of its truth by a conscious and deliberate investigation of its truth-value. Assurance is possible without consequentially rational belief. You can assure yourself that *p* without even having that purely local

[1] Cf. Swinburne (1968)
[2] Levi (1954) Chs. 3 and 4

mode of consequentially rational belief that *p* in which you consider nothing but the intrinsic value of true belief when you evaluate the outcomes of believing and not believing *p*. Even if the man who assures himself that *p* sees an intrinsic value in believing the truth, he need not compare the outcomes of believing and not believing *p* in order to satisfy himself that *p* is true. Equally, assuring yourself that *p*, unlike being consequentially rational in believing it, is not consistent with believing that *p* is less probable than *not-p*. The simplest case of consequentially rational belief in a proposition believed to be less probable than its negation would be of a purely local mode, involving the consideration of nothing but the intrinsic value of believing the truth. You would need to believe that believing *p* when *p* is true is very much better than any of the other three possible outcomes of believing and not believing *p*, and that *p* is only a little less probable than its negation.

Just as assurance is possible without consequentially rational belief, so consequentially rational belief is possible without assurance. And yet, if consequentially rational belief is to avoid all arbitrariness, there must, I think, be some proposition which you assure yourself to be true. If you are consequentially rational in believing *p* then you believe certain propositions about outcomes of believing and not believing *p*: that such and such possible outcomes have such and such a value, perhaps also that they have such and such a probability. Let us call these propositions about outcomes O-propositions. If, in the calculations which made your belief that *p* consequentially rational, the O-propositions are not just arbitrarily accepted, then it seems that you must either be consequentially rational in believing them or have assured yourself of their truth. Let us consider the first alternative, that you are consequentially rational in believing the O-propositions. How do you decide which outcomes of believing and not believing the O-propositions to evaluate? If your interest in the consequential rationality of your belief in the O-propositions derives from your desire to have a wholly non-arbitrary kind of consequentially rational belief that *p*, then it would be odd not to include precisely the realisation of that desire as a possible outcome of your believing the O-propositions. But, on our first alternative, this is not a possible outcome of your believing the O-propositions, unless you are consequentially rational in believing the O-propositions. And you cannot be consequentially rational in believing the O-propositions except by believing among other things that the realisation of your desire for a wholly non-arbitrary consequentially rational belief that *p* is a possible outcome of believing the *O*-propositions. Our first alternative seems then to require the arbitrary belief that something is possible which would not be possible unless you believed it was. There are no similar difficulties with the second alternative, which is that you have assured yourself that the *O*-propositions are true, without being consequentially rational in believing them. We can say then that assurance of truth is not merely distinct from, but also in a certain way required by, consequentially rational belief.

(2) *Assurance of truth*

To assure yourself that a proposition is true is consciously and deliberately to do something which satisfies you of its truth. Assurance can be either evidential or experiential. You evidentially assure yourself that *p* only if you consciously affirm a proposition which you consciously affirm to be evidence for *p*. You experientially assure yourself that *p* when your satisfaction of *p*'s truth is gained directly from your experience, and the proposition that you have this experience is not one which you both consciously affirm and consciously affirm to be evidence for *p*. So for example you might evidentially assure yourself that there is coal in the cellar by reflecting that the last delivery was in November and that you usually burn about two sacks a week, and experientially assure yourself that there is coal in the cellar by deciding to go down and see, opening the cellar door, and then seeing a large pile of it in the corner. In both cases there is a conscious and deliberate activity of investigation; but there is no question, in the experiential case, of your actually affirming that you had a visual experience as of coal, that you were sober at the time, etc., etc.

Necessarily, you believe *p* on completing the operation of assuring yourself that *p*. And if we admit partial belief, as a state bounded by belief and disbelief, we can also introduce the notion of partially assuring yourself that *p*, an operation issuing in a partial belief that *p*, and bounded by assuring yourself that *p* and assuring yourself that *p*'s truth is neither more nor less likely than its falsity. Maybe, not having actually got up from your arm-chair and trying to work everything out from the last delivery date, you can only reach partial assurance that there is still some coal in the cellar.

If you have assured yourself that p, then you are sure that p. But the converse relation does not hold, since something can make you sure that p even though you have not yourself consciously and deliberately investigated p's truth-value. There is also a distinction between having assured yourself that p and having been assured that p by someone else. 'He assured me that he was a Belgian, but I still didn't believe it' is consistent; 'I assured myself that he was a Belgian, but I still didn't believe it' is not consistent. In what follows 'N is assured that p' and 'N has assurance that p' will be used so that they are true only if N has assured himself that p, by an investigation which may or may not take account of someone else's testimony; it will not be sufficient for their truth that an assurance that p has been issued by someone else and understood by N.

This section is mostly about experiential assurance. Various theses and further terminological conventions are established, which I shall need to appeal to when arguing later for the scarcity and desirability of radical assurance. There will be a more detailed treatment of evidential assurance, with a similar general aim, in section (3).

My initial coal-cellar example was of gaining experiential assurance that p by actually seeing that p. But of course actually seeing that p is not necessary for gaining even that experiential assurance of p's truth in which the experience is visual. You can still assure yourself even if you are unlucky enough to be having an illusion. Nor is seeing that p sufficient for experientially assuring yourself of p's truth. Seeing that p must be the intended upshot of a conscious and deliberate activity of investigation. You can see that there is a dandelion in the field without having consciously *done* anything at all, without having decided to investigate anything, without that standing back from and reflection about a proposition which is a necessary prelude to assuring yourself of its truth. So a man can see, and indeed be sure, that p, and yet either have no assurance that p, or, if he does have assurance, have assurance of a purely evidential kind. (Austin, in his anxiety to insist that there could be seeing without having evidence, went so far as to suggest that one cannot have evidence for p when one actually sees that p is true. 'The situation in which I would properly be said to have *evidence* for the statement that some animal is a pig is that, for example, in which the beast itself is not actually on view, but I can see plenty of pig-like marks

on the ground outside its retreat.'[1] But someone who saw that *p*
might be sophisticated enough to reflect that it looked to him as if *p*
and that this proposition about his visual experience was evidence
for *p*.)

There is nothing to stop you from simultaneously having both
evidential and experiential assurance that one and the same proposition is true. If you see your sister when you get back upstairs from
the cellar and she says 'Of course there is coal left', it is neither
logically nor psychologically impossible for you tediously to seize
the opportunity to assure yourself all over again: 'She *did* say it',
'She *is* trustworthy', etc., etc. What my definitions really do rule out
is that you should have experientially assured yourself that there is
coal in the cellar by an activity of investigation which ends in visual
experience, and at the same time have an evidential assurance in
which the evidence you affirm is that you had a visual experience as
of coal.

Given these definitions, all assurance is either evidential or
experiential. This is the first main thesis I want to put forward in
this section, and it is I think a contingent truth. A likely objection
would be this. Suppose someone assures himself that *p* is true by a
deliberate investigation which ends in experience, and then consciously affirms the proposition that he has had this experience and
that the proposition that he has had it is evidence for *p*. His affirmation of these propositions makes his assurance non-experiential, on
my definition. But might he not owe his satisfaction of *p*'s truth
solely to the investigation ending in experience and not to his
affirmation of these propositions about his experience? If so, then
his assurance would also be non-evidential, on my definition. The
case seems to me psychologically impossible. If he affirms the
propositions then this gives him either a full or a partial evidential
assurance which displaces his previous experiential assurance. If I
satisfy myself that there is coal in the cellar by deciding to go and
see, and then seeing some, but then subsequently recognise that I
had a visual experience as of coal and that the proposition that I had
this experience is evidence for there being coal in the cellar, my
experiential assurance does not survive this recognition, and any
assurance I subsequently have will be evidential. There is an analogy, perhaps, in the way that your indeterminate conviction that
there is something odd about her face would not survive your more

[1] Austin (1962) p. 115

specific recognition that one of her eyes is a slightly different colour from the other.

To say that all assurance is evidential or experiential is not of course to say anything about what actual kinds of experience we enjoy, not to commit oneself on the existence or otherwise of inner as well as outer sensory experience, or even on the existence or otherwise of experience of a wholly non-sensory kind.

It will be convenient at this point to introduce some more special terminology. Firstly, then, I will talk of experience as having an intentional object. To talk in this way is neither to explain anything nor to commit oneself to any daring ontological doctrine. To say that someone is having an experience with an intentional object is to say no more than that he is having an experience which we cannot completely characterise except by describing what it is of, and such that we can describe what it is of without implying either that it is true or that it is false that what it is of exists independently of the experience itself. To say that someone is having an experience whose intentional object is a scarlet poppy, or whose intentional object is scarlet and physical, is not to imply that, whether or not there is an independently existing scarlet physical object, there is at any rate an object, dependent for its existence on the occurrence of the experience, which is itself somehow scarlet and quasi-physical and itself perceived or experienced.[1] It is however still convenient to talk of resemblances between the intentional objects of experiences and states of affairs existing independently of these experiences. An F is the intentional object of the experience one would describe by saying that he has a visual impression of an F. And we can say that there is a resemblance between the intentional object of this experience and an independently existing state of affairs 'There is an H' if 'There is an F' implies 'There is a G' and, were there an independently existing state of affairs describable as 'There is a G', that state of affairs would resemble or be identical to the independently existing state of affairs 'There is an H'. Suppose for example that I am having a veridical visual experience whose intentional object is a scarlet poppy before me. If 'There is a scarlet poppy before me' implies both 'There is an inherently scarlet object before me' and 'There is a physical object before me' then there is a resemblance between the intentional object of my experience and the independently existing states of affairs 'There is an inherently scarlet object before me' and

[1] See Mackie (1976) pp. 47–51

'There is a physical object before me.' If on the other hand 'scarlet' is the name of a secondary property, so that 'There is a scarlet poppy before me' does not imply 'There is an inherently scarlet object before me', it still implies 'There is a physical object before me', and there is still a resemblance between the intentional object of my experience and the independently existing state of affairs 'There is a physical object before me.'

Secondly, I shall say that the intentional object of an experience is inner if the experience is of or as of a state of or change in the experiencer's own mind, and otherwise outer. And I shall say that the intentional object of an experience is concrete if the experience is of or as of something located in either space or time, and otherwise abstract. The restrictive-looking thesis that all assurance is evidential or experiential implies nothing about whether we have sensory experiences whose intentional objects are inner, as well as sensory experience with outer intentional objects. It implies nothing about whether there are mystical or other non-sensory experiences whose intentional objects are outer and concrete. And it implies nothing about whether there is such a thing as the metaphorical 'seeing' of traditional rationalism, construed either as involving experience whose intentional object is outer or abstract, or as the experience of acquiring, by means other than sensory experience or reflection on evidence, an especially powerful conviction.

The other main thesis I want to put forward in this section is about whether the gaining of experiential assurance is compatible with consciousness of the nature of the activity by which it has been gained.

Let 'sensory assurance' be our label for experiential assurance in which the terminating experience is gained through the operation of inner or outer senses and has an intentional object which at least partially resembles what is stated to be so by the proposition of whose truth the subject is experientially assured. And let 'intuitive assurance' be our label for experiential assurance in which the terminating experience is merely that of acquiring a powerful conviction of the truth of the proposition of whose truth the subject is experientially assured. Assume that hallucination, illusion, and the veridical perception of an independently existing state of affairs all require the subject to have experience, and that in both the veridical and the illusory perception of an independently existing state of affairs there is at least some resemblance between this state of affairs and the intentional object of the experience. Assume further that a proposition to the effect that someone is having an experience is at least evidence for, even though it may not entail, a proposition to the effect that there is an independently existing state of affairs to which the intentional object of the experience bears some resemblance. If 'scarlet' is the name of a secondary quality, then the proposition that someone is having an experience whose intentional object is a scarlet poppy will not be evidence that there is an independently existing and inherently scarlet flower, but only evidence for the existence of an independently existing object which bears some other resemblance to the intentional object of his visual experience, e.g. resembles it *qua* physical object. If triangularity is a primary quality then the proposition that someone is having an experience whose intentional object is a triangular piece of metal will be evidence for the independent existence of an inherently triangular physical object. These assumptions are I hope as innocent as my initial introduction of intentional objects. They do not, for example, oblige me to take sides on whether or not it is true, either contingently or necessarily, that in the veridical sensory perception of an independently existing state of affairs the subject's sensory experience is caused by that state of affairs.

Given these definitions and assumptions, I suggest that experientially assuring yourself that *p* is incompatible with consciousness of the nature of the activity by means of which your assurance has been gained if your assurance is sensory, but compatible if your assurance is intuitive. Suppose you assure yourself that *p* is true by an activity of investigation which ends in sensory experience. Then, as I am assuming, the proposition that you have this sensory experience is evidence for the independent existence of a state of affairs which does or does not bear a resemblance to the intentional object of the experience which is sufficiently close for the experiential proposition to be evidence for *p*. And this is something that you will recognise if you are conscious of the nature of your investigatory activity. If, in recognising this, you decide that the resemblance between the intentional and the independently existing object is too small for the experiential proposition to be evidence for *p* at all, then you will no longer be in any way assured that *p*. If on the other hand you decide that the resemblance between the intentional and the independently existing object is sufficient for the experiential proposition to be evidence for *p*, then you will still not continue to have *sensory* assurance that *p*. For as we have already seen (see pp. 18–19 above), it is impossible for someone to be simultaneously assured of the truth of *p* both by having an experience, and by reflecting that the proposition that he has this experience is both true and evidence for *p*. No parallel dilemma is applicable to intuitive assurance, that species of experiential assurance in which the experience is merely the consciousness of acquiring, by means other than the reflection on evidence or sensory experience, an especially powerful conviction. For it is no evidence for the truth of a proposition that someone believes it, however powerful his conviction may be. And so if you say that someone who has intuitively assured himself that *p* becomes conscious of the nature of the activity by which he gained this assurance you are not forced into saying that he will then believe something about evidence which will either make his assurance that *p* evidential or destroy it altogether. Consciousness of the nature of the activity by means of which you have gained experiential assurance is compatible with the continued existence of an originally intuitive assurance but not compatible with the continued existence of an originally sensory assurance. And there is a similar opposition between this self-consciousness and the continued existence of any non-sensory and non-intuitive experiential assurance which we may be able to gain.

This last thesis, like the thesis that all assurance is evidential or experiential, will become clearer when I apply it to questions about the scarcity and desirability of radical assurance. Before coming to that, however, I must say something more about evidential assurance. And the first step here is to consider evidential relations between propositions.

(3) *Evidence and evidential assurance*

The notion of evidence which I use in this book is a liberalised version of what I take to be the ordinary notion of evidence. *q* is evidence for *p* only if (i) *q* is true; (ii) when a proposition like *q* is true so usually at least is a proposition like *p*; (iii) it is not the case that when a proposition like *not-q* is true so usually at least is a proposition like *p*, or, better perhaps, (iiia) there is an explanatory connexion between *q* and *p*; and (iv) a normally intelligent man with antecedent doubts about the truth of *p* would not thereby be made equally doubtful about the truth of *q*. These four conditions give us a rough description of the ordinary notion of evidence. In the liberalised notion I want to use, condition (i) is no longer necessary. But before saying what makes this change convenient, I must say a little about the four conditions governing the ordinary notion itself.

That q must be true in order to be in an ordinary sense evidence for p is, I think, uncontentious. If Joe did not actually say that the garden is overgrown, then even if he does usually tell the truth you would not say ' "Joe says the garden is overgrown" is evidence for "the garden is overgrown".' You would say 'If Joe had said that the garden was overgrown that would have been evidence for its being overgrown.'

How can condition (ii) be made more precise? The requirement might be that there should be two classes of propositions Q and P such that q belongs to Q and p to P, and one–one mapping of Q into P such that usually at least when an element of Q is true so also is its image in P. So for example it is a necessary condition for 'Arthur knows Greek' to be in the ordinary sense evidence for 'Arthur knows Latin', that when any particular member of the class of propositions predicating a knowledge of Greek of some individual is true, so usually at least is that member of the class of propositions predicating a knowledge of Latin which predicates this knowledge of the same individual who is credited with a knowledge of Greek by the proposition of the first class. In this example q and p are merely contingently related. But it is also possible for q to be evidence for p when q entails p. In this sort of case there will be classes Q and P and a mapping of Q into P such that it is necessarily true that when an element of Q is true so also is its image in P. And it may also be possible for q to be evidence for p when q is non-contingently related to p without entailing it. There may be classes Q and P and a mapping of Q into P such that it is necessarily true that when an element of Q is true so usually but not always is its image in P. It is a necessary condition for the existence of so called criterial evidence that (ii) should be satisfiable in this way (see p. 144 below). If P and Q are finite sets, then there is no problem about the meaning of 'usually at least when an element of Q is true so also is its image in P'. But what could this mean if P and Q were infinite? We would need to bring in the notion of limiting frequency in a random sequence. If C is that subset of the Cartesian product of P and Q which is given by the mapping of Q into P, and C_1 that subset of C whose elements are ordered pairs whose first member is true, then if the elements of C_1 were arranged in a random sequence, the limiting frequency of ordered pairs whose second member was also true would be over a half.

If conditions (i) and (ii) were jointly sufficient then if q were true it could be evidence for p merely because p is the sort of proposition which is usually or always true anyway. Since people hardly ever live to be 140, 'Arthur is interested in the history of Sweden' would, if it happened to be true, be evidence for 'Arthur will not live to be 140', and likewise evidence for any necessarily true proposition you care to choose. One way of ruling out counter-examples of this kind is to insist that (iii) it is not the case that when a proposition like *not-q* is true so usually at least is a proposition like p, i.e. that it is not the case that (ii) is also satisfied by *not-q* and p. Thus if q is 'Arthur is interested in the history of Sweden' and p is 'Arthur will not live to be 140' or 'If anything is red it is coloured' then if q is true, q and p satisfy (i) and (ii). But still q will not be evidence for p, because it is also true that when a proposition like 'Arthur is not interested in the history of Sweden' is true so usually is a proposition like 'Arthur will not live to be 140', and so always is a proposition like 'If anything is red it is coloured'.

But if (iii) prevents us from having to say that any true proposition is evidence for any necessary proposition, there is also the danger that it will rule out evidence for necessary propositions altogether. The premises in Euclid's proof that there is no greatest prime number are presumably evidence for the conclusion, but since the conclusion is necessarily true, will it not also be the case that propositions like it are always true even when propositions like the negation of the conjunction of the premises are true? And even if that supposition is senseless, because the conjunction of the premises in Euclid's proof is itself necessary, is it not at least logically possible that a contingent proposition is evidence for a necessary proposition? The fact that p is necessary does not seem to make 'Most of what N says is true and N says that p' any the less evidence for p.

Faced with these difficulties, you may prefer to replace (iii) by the requirement that (iiia) there is an explanatory connection between q and p. Or more specifically, to insist that q is evidence for p only if either q explains p, or p explains q or there is a third, and true, proposition which explains both q and p. Something of this sort is suggested by Achinstein. There are according to him two distinct every-day and scientific concepts of an evidential relation between propositions. *e* is potential evidence that *h* if and only if (a) *e* is true, (b) *e* does not entail *h*, (c) $Pr(h, e) > k$, (d) Pr (there is an explanatory connexion between *h* and *e*, $h.e) > k$, where $Pr(h, e)$ is high if $> k$. And *e* is veridical evidence that *h* if and only if '*e* is potential evidence that *h*, *h* is true and there is an explanatory connexion between the truth of *h* and *e*'.[1] Achinstein, with his condition (b), is presumably prepared to say that the premises in an acceptable mathematical proof are at least sometimes not evidence for its conclusion. And if we reject this restriction we will of course need to take 'explanatory connexion' in a rather wide sense, appeal to a genus explanation of which chronological explanation, or the explanation of why an event occurs when it does, is merely one of several species. To explain something, in this generic sense, could be simply to make it intellectually plain (planus), open and surveyable. Why some event occurs when it does could be explained by sub-suming the event under a causal or statistical law, what some lump of matter is by the description of its ingredients, what some sequence of sounds is by the description of the thoughts it is conventionally taken to express, what some proposition is by the exhibition of con-ditions logically necessary and sufficient for its truth. We can then say that 'Arthur is interested in the history of Sweden' fails to be evidence for 'Arthur will not live to be 140' because of the lack of even a chronologically explanatory relation between the two propositions, and 'Arthur is interested in the history of Sweden' fails to be evidence for 'If anything is red it is coloured', of the sort which Euclid gave for the proposition that there exists an infinity of prime numbers, because propositions about Arthur are not logically necessary for the truth of 'If anything is red it is coloured'.

Not that (iiia) is without its own difficulties. When *q* and *p* are both contingent, the requirement of an explanatory connexion seems unnecessarily strong. If 'The ice is melting' is evidence for 'The temperature has begun to rise' then perhaps we can causally explain the first proposition in terms of the second, but so long as the first proposition is true, and when a proposition like it is true so usually at least is a proposition like the second, then that seems enough for it to be evidence for the second, whether or not there are also the hidden mechanisms, natural necessities or whatever which

[1] Achinstein (1978) p. 35

causal explanation is supposed additionally to require. It is not clear, either, that an explanatory connexion requirement is satisfied by q and p when q is of the form 'Most of what N says is true and N says that p'.

But however exactly we develop either (iii) or (iiia), it seems unlikely that we will end up with something whose conjunction with (i) and (ii) is sufficient for q to be evidence for p, because to call q evidence for p is to talk not just about the explanatory relations between the two propositions, or the relations between their truth-values, but also about the role which the contemplation of q can be expected to play in the alleviation of a person's antecedent doubts about p's truth. q is evidence for p only if (iv) a normally intelligent man with antecedent doubts about p's truth would not thereby be made at least equally doubtful about the truth of q. Since q strictly implies 'q or r', conditions (i) and (ii) are satisfied whenever q is true and p is a disjunction of which q is a member. Nor, when q and p are related in that way, is there any reason why they should not also satisfy condition (iii). But it seems wrong to say that a proposition is evidence for a disjunction of which it is itself a member, and this, I take it, is because any normally intelligent person doubtful about the truth of the disjunction would thereby be made equally doubtful about the truth of each of its disjuncts. (iiia) might admittedly exclude this case; there does at any rate seem no sense, chronological or otherwise, in which a disjunction explains or is explained by one of its disjuncts. But (i), (ii) and (iiia) might be satisfied by q and p if q was of the form 'not *not-p*', and it would be equally absurd to say that under this interpretation q was evidence for p.

Does condition (iv) come down to the requirement that the argument 'q therefore p' should not be question-begging? Your argument is question-begging, as addressed to some particular person with antecedent doubts about the truth of the proposition which forms its conclusion, if, in advancing your argument, you are in effect asking him to grant you, as a premiss, the very proposition whose truth is the question at issue between you. But as Hamblin notes, 'the name "Begging the Question" is often extended to cases in which, although the precise point in dispute is not itself assumed as a premiss, something equally questionable is assumed in its place'. Thus 'Whately . . . defines it as that "in which one of the premisses is either manifestly the same in sense with the conclusion, or is actually proved from it, or is such as the persons you are addressing are not likely to know, or to admit, except as an inference from the conclusion".'[1] And we could I think capture this extended sense by saying that an argument is question-begging, as addressed to some particular person with antecedent doubts about its conclusion, if by actually having these doubts he is made equally doubtful about one or more of its premises. If this is right then condition (iv) comes down to the requirement that the argument '*q* therefore *p*' should not be question-begging as addressed to any normally intelligent man with antecedent doubts about its conclusion, or, as we can say, not normally question-begging. Condition (iv) does not prevent *q* from being evidence for *p*, even though the argument in which it is presented to somebody as evidence for *p* is made question-begging by the particular beliefs which that person holds. 'Charlotte says that capitalism will collapse and she is never wrong about anything', can be evidence for 'capitalism will collapse' even if the corresponding argument happens to be question-begging as addressed to me. As it happens, there is nothing to prevent my uncertainties about the future of capitalism from making me equally doubtful about Charlotte's alleged infallibility. But things would have been different if I had had an unshakeable and antecedent conviction of her infallibility. An argument of the form '*q* therefore *q*', '*q* therefore (*q* or *r*)', or '(*r* and *p*) therefore *p*' is on the other hand normally question-begging. So, by (iv), a proposition cannot be evidence for itself, or for a disjunction of which it is itself a disjunct, or for one of its own conjuncts. Nor, by the same condition, can evidence for *p* be of the form 'not *not-p*', or of the form '(*not-r* or *p*) and *r*'.

I shall take it then that *q* is in the ordinary sense evidence for *p* if and only if conditions (i), (ii) and (iv) and something like (iii) or (iiia) are satisfied. Nothing hangs for my purposes on how exactly the difficulties arising out of (iii) and (iiia) are met.

I said earlier that you are evidentially assured that *p* only if you consciously affirm a proposition *q* which you consciously affirm to be evidence for *p*. There is a redundancy here, if 'evidence' is taken in its ordinary sense, for since *q* must obviously be true in order to be evidence for *p*, you affirm *q* in affirming that it is evidence for *p*. But sceptical questions arise about whether you can and must be assured that *q* is evidence for *p*, in order to be evidentially assured that *p*. These difficulties divide naturally into difficulties about assurance that *q* is true and assurances that *q* and *p* satisfy the

[1] Hamblin (1970) p. 34

remaining conditions necessary for the evidential relation. And it is for the sake of this division that I shall use 'evidence', from now onwards, in a liberalised sense in which q is evidence for p only if (ii)–(iv) are satisfied, but in which it is not necessary that (i) q is true. In this liberalised sense of 'evidence', only difficulties about the satisfaction of conditions (ii)–(iv) are difficulties about whether q is evidence for p, and difficulties about (i) are about the separate question of whether q is true. There is, similarly, no redundancy in the formula 'N is evidentially assured that p only if he consciously affirms a proposition which he consciously affirms to be evidence for p', when 'evidence' is taken in the liberalised sense.

In addition to the necessary conditions (ii)–(iv), there are one or two features, common to both the ordinary and the liberalised senses of 'evidence', which I shall need to invoke later on in my argument. Firstly, if p is a conjunction, then 'q is evidence for p' entails 'q is evidence for each conjunct of p'. Secondly, the relation 'is evidence for' is not necessarily transitive. To see this we can suppose that (a) 'One of the faces 1, 2, 3, 4, 5 will turn up' is evidence for (b) 'One of the faces 1, 2, 3, 4 will turn up.' which is in turn evidence for (c) 'One of the faces 1, 2, 3 will turn up' which is in turn evidence for (d) 'One of the faces 1, 2 will turn up'. It by no means follows that (a) is evidence for (d). Finally, the relation 'is evidence for' is not asymmetrical. It is perfectly possible for there to be two propositions q and p such that when a proposition like q is true so usually at least is a proposition like p, and when a proposition like p is true so usually at least is a proposition like q. And there can perfectly well be two sets of circumstances, in one of which your doubts about p's truth do not make you equally doubtful about q's truth, and in the other of which your doubts about q's truth do not make you equally doubtful about p's truth. In one set of circumstances recognising that the creature has a heart might make you more confident that it has kidneys, in another set of circumstances recognising that it has kidneys might make you more confident that it has a heart. What is impossible, however, is that you should be evidentially assured that p by adducing q as evidence for p and at the same time evidentially assured that q by adducing p as evidence for q. If it is your conviction that the creature has a heart which makes you evidentially assured that it has kidneys, it cannot also be your conviction that it has kidneys which makes you evidentially assured that it has a heart. It is not the evidential relation between two propositions which is asymmetrical, but the relation which holds between being evidentially assured that p and being evidentially assured that q when you are evidentially assured that p by adducing q as evidence for p, or more generally, the relation between being evidentially assured that p and being evidentially assured that q, when you are evidentially assured that p by adducing q as evidence either for p or for a proposition which you adduce as evidence for p, or . . . etc.[1]

It is a necessary condition for being evidentially assured that p that you consciously affirm a proposition which you consciously affirm to be evidence for p. But the condition is not sufficient. For one thing, you might perfectly well also affirm a proposition which you affirm to be evidence for *not-p*. It is perfectly possible, and perhaps even usual, for a proposition to be such that there is both a true proposition which is evidence for it, and a true proposition which is evidence for its negation. Suppose p is 'Arthur knows Latin', q is 'Arthur knows Greek' and q_1 is 'Arthur is an engineer'. Then if most people who know Greek also know Latin but most engineers do not know Latin, we can say both that q is true and evidence for p, and that q_1 is true and evidence for *not-p*. More generally, any propositions q and p will each belong to an indefinite number of classes of propositions $Q_1, Q_2, Q_3, \ldots$ and $P_1, P_2, P_3, \ldots$ and there will almost always be three classes of propositions Q_1, Q_2, and P_1 such that q belongs to both Q_1 and Q_2, and p to P_1, and there is a one–one mapping of Q_1 into P_1 such that usually at least when an element of Q_1 is true so also is its image in P_1, and a one–one mapping of Q_2 into P_1 such that usually at least when an element of Q_2 is true its image in P_1 is false. This means that when q and p stand in the relation required by condition (ii) so almost always will q and *not-p*. And there is no reason why this should not remain true even if q and p are true propositions which satisfy conditions (iii) and (iv).

This makes it useful to introduce the notion of overriding evidence. q is overriding evidence for p if it is stronger evidence for p than any true proposition is for *not-p*. And it is a necessary condition for being evidentially assured that p that you consciously affirm a proposition which you consciously affirm to be overriding evidence for p. By the definition of overriding evidence, it is not possible for a proposition to be such that there is both a true

[1] Cf. Jaeger (1975)

proposition which is overriding evidence for it and a true proposition which is overriding evidence for its negation. I take it that q's strength, as evidence for p, depends partly on its weight or extent, and partly on the strength of the truth-correlations between p and each of those components of q which determine its weight or extent. Suppose for example that p is 'the light was on at midnight'. If X and Y are each fairly reliable, then the conjunction 'X said the light was on at midnight and Y said the light was on at midnight' will be weightier or more extensive evidence for p than 'X said the light was on at midnight'. But the strength of the conjunction, as evidence for p, depends also on how reliable X and Y are, e.g. on how often it is that when a proposition like 'X said the light was on at midnight' is true, so also is a proposition like p.

A word now on my usage of 'p is probably true' and 'q is a reason for believing p'. 'q is evidence for p' and 'q is a reason for believing p' are often used as simple equivalents. But 'q is a reason for believing p' is ambiguous in ordinary usage. A reason for believing p can either be evidence for p, in the ordinary sense which I earlier tried to describe, or the sort of proposition about the values and perhaps also probabilities of the outcomes of believing p and not believing p whose truth makes it a good thing to be in the state of believing p, regardless of whether there is any evidence for p. A reason for believing p, in this latter sense, is the sort of proposition which you must believe in order to be what I called consequentially rational in believing p (see p. 9 above). If the calculations in Pascal's wager are correct, then there is a reason, in this latter sense, for believing in the existence of God, even if there is no proposition which is in the ordinary sense evidence that God exists. It may be that we sometimes make it part of the meaning of 'q is a reason for believing p' *both* that usually when a proposition like q is true so also is a proposition like p *and* that if q is known then it is in some normative sense right to believe p. Thus Blackburn, in his study of the problem of induction, analyses 'q is a reason for p' as 'it is right to have more confidence in p upon coming to know q than before coming to know q, or would be right to do this if not already certain that p is true or that p is false, or as certain as evidence like p can make one'[1] and at the same time takes it as necessarily true that using a reason is 'an operation which generally yields the truth'.[2] What I need, however,

[1] Blackburn (1973) p. 23 (p and q transposed)
[2] ibid. p. 41

is a terminology which emphasises the distinction between three different types of question: about truth-correlations between propositions, about the activities by which a man assures himself of a proposition's truth, and about the comparative moral or other value of states of believing. I therefore reserve 'reason for believing p' as a label for the sort of proposition which you have to believe in order for your believing of p to be consequentially rational, and leave 'evidence for p' to stand for what is truth-correlated with p and has to be taken as such in one method of reaching assurance that p is true.

Finally, 'p is probably true'. The most natural everyday sense of 'probable' and 'likely', according to Mackie, can be indicated by saying 'that "probably P" or "it is likely that P" means something like "it is reasonable to believe that P, but the reasons are inconclusive"'.[1] And he later describes 'one extreme' of this informal concept as follows: 'to say that it is probable that P is to say that there are good, but not conclusive reasons for believing that P'.[2] If we take 'reason for believing that p' as 'evidence for p', then this last explanation of Mackie's gives a rough idea of how 'p is probably true' will be used in what follows. More precisely, 'p is probably true' will mean that there is a true proposition q which is overriding evidence for p but does not entail p. I note that if p is a proposition to the effect that some other proposition p_1 is probably true, then 'q is overriding evidence for p' will not entail 'q is true and overriding evidence for p_1'. 'q is overriding evidence for p' will on this interpretation of 'p' mean only that q is overriding evidence for the existence of some true proposition or other which is overriding evidence for p_1 but does not entail it; the true proposition in question does not have to be identical to q.

With this much said about evidence, I want now to look a little more closely at the notion of evidential assurance. I made it a necessary condition for evidentially assuring yourself of p's truth that you consciously affirm a proposition q which you consciously affirm to be overriding evidence for p. But even this condition is not sufficient. You may perfectly well affirm that q is stronger evidence for p than any true proposition for *not-p* and yet think that q is not very strong evidence for p. In this case you may only be able to reach partial evidential assurance that p (see p. 16 above). And your degree of evidential assurance that p may depend not merely on how

[1] Mackie (1973) p. 156   [2] ibid. p. 159

strong you think the evidence is which you adduce in p's favour, but also on the degree of assurance you have that this evidence is true, and the degree of assurance you have that it is evidence of a certain strength. A proper theory of evidential assurance would elucidate all these factors, and also answer such questions as whether, in having that greater or lesser degree of belief that q which is relevant to your degree of evidential assurance that p, you believe that q is more or less probable in a sense which conforms to the axioms of the classical calculus of probabilities.[1] But I do not aim to develop a theory of evidential assurance for its own sake, and none of my subsequent arguments about radical assurance would be affected by the more specific conclusions about partial assurance and the scope of classical probability which such a theory would need to reach. The feature of evidential assurance which I really do need to attend to is what we can call its degree of regressiveness. Some remarks on this notion will finally put me in a position to define radical assurance itself.

A man can evidentially assure himself that p is true even though he has assured himself neither that q is true, nor that q is evidence for p. He can assure himself that Quito is the capital of Ecuador by affirming that he read it in an encyclopaedia, and that the encyclopaedia is reliable, even though he does not take any steps to assure himself either that he did read it there or that the encyclopaedia is in fact reliable. This is a case in which the man is in the weakest sense evidentially assured that p. A stronger notion of evidential assurance that p would require you to have assured yourself of the truth either of the proposition q which you affirm to be overriding evidence for p or of the proposition that q is overriding evidence for p. A still stronger notion would require you to assure yourself of the truth of both these propositions but if your assurance that q was evidential not require you to assure yourself of the truth of both the proposition q_1 which you affirm to be overriding evidence for q, and the proposition that q_1 is overriding evidence for q. And so on. By degree of regressiveness I mean degree of strength on this scale. We will see in the next section that radical assurance is on this scale maximally strong, or, as I shall say, ultra-regressive. Evidential assurance is ultra-regressive only if a certain infinite series of conditions is satisfied. The following diagram represents the first few members of the series, and shows how to go from there.

[1] See Cohen (1977) Part II

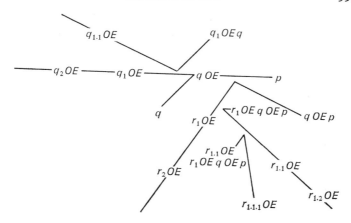

The line from p to qOE represents the condition, necessary for being evidentially assured that p, that you have assured yourself that q is overriding evidence for p. The lines from qOE to q and to q_1OE represent the necessary condition that you have assured yourself that q: the line from qOE to q represents the possibility that this assurance is non-evidential, and the line from qOE to q_1OE represents the possibility that this assurance is evidential and involves the affirmation that q_1 is overriding evidence for p. From the line joining qOE to q_1OE there are lines to q_1OEq and to to $q_{1·1}OE$. These represent the condition that if your assurance that q is evidential, then you have assured yourself that q_1 is overriding evidence for q: the line to q_1OEq represents the possibility that this latter assurance is non-evidential, and the line to $q_{1·1}OE$ represents the possibility that this latter assurance is evidential. From the line joining p and qOE there are lines to $qOEp$ and to r_1OE. These represent the necessary condition that you have assured yourself that q is overriding evidence for p: the line to $qOEp$ represents the possibility that this assurance is non-evidential, and the line to r_1OE represents the possibility that this assurance is evidential and involves the affirmation that r_1 is overriding evidence for 'q is overriding evidence for p'.

(4) *Radical assurance*

Assurance, on the thesis of section (2), must be either evidential or experiential. And I have now said something about each of these two kinds of assurance. I come next to the distinction between radical and non-radical assurance, which cuts across the division into evidential and experiential kinds.

You are radically assured that p if and only if (i) you have assured yourself that p; (ii) p is true; (iii) if your assurance that p is evidential then it is ultra-regressive; (iv) on gaining your assurance that p, you are conscious of the nature of the activity of investigation by means of which your assurance has been gained; (v) there is a non-coincidental relation between your activity of gaining assurance that p and the fact that in believing p you are believing what is true; and (vi) if your assurance that p is evidential then conditions (i)–(v) would still hold if we substituted for p any of those additional propositions whose truth you must be assured of in order for condition (iii) to be satisfied. The previous discussion will I hope have illuminated the meaning of (i) and (iii). You will be curious about the non-coincidental relation of condition (v). But actually nothing much hangs for my purposes on precisely how (v) is satisfied. It would do to suppose that in investigating p's truth-value, you put yourself into a position in which you are caused to believe p by what makes p true. It would also do to suppose that there is a harmony between your activity of investigation and what makes p true which is independent of any asymmetrical relation between what makes p true and the fact that believing p terminates your investigations.

Although radical assurance can be either evidential or experiential, it can only be experiential if it is intuitive, i.e. if the terminating experience is merely that of acquiring a powerful conviction of the truth of the proposition of whose truth the subject is experientially assured (see p. 20 above). The exclusively intuitive nature of experiential radical assurance follows from the conjunction of condition (iv) and a thesis of section (2). According to condition (iv), you are radically assured that p only if, on gaining your assurance that p, you are conscious of the nature of the activity of investigation by means of which your assurance has been gained. And the section (2) thesis is that consciousness of the nature of the activity by means of which you have gained experiential assurance is compatible with the continued existence of an originally intuitive assurance, but not compatible with the continued existence of an originally sensory or otherwise non-intuitive experiential assurance. Given the other main thesis of section (2), which is that all assurance is evidential or experiential, it follows that all radical assurance is evidential or intuitive. And this, as I will show in the next chapter, places a very severe constraint on the actual scope of radical assurance, at least if we assume no more about the scope of intuitive assurance than you are likely to be willing to assume.

But before coming on to the limits of radical assurance, more needs to be said about its actual nature. In the rest of this section, I will draw some general comparisons with other cognitive concepts. In the next section of the chapter I will look more closely at radical and intuitive assurance, and at what you will be willing to assume about the scope of intuitive assurance in general.

How, to begin with, is radical assurance related to knowledge? Having radical assurance that *p* is probably sufficient for knowing that *p*. If we are prepared to call justified true belief knowledge when there is a non-coincidental relation between what makes the proposition believed true and what makes the believing of it justified, and if justified believing can be identified in this context with having an assurance of truth, then having radical assurance that *p* is sufficient for knowing that *p*. For if you are radically assured that *p*, then you believe *p*, *p* is true, and there is a non-coincidental relation between your activity of assuring yourself that *p* and the fact that in believing *p* you are believing what is true.

But having assured yourself that *p*, radically or otherwise, is clearly not necessary for knowing that *p*. Knowing does not require a conscious and deliberate activity of investigation. There may for instance be a sort of knowing which consists simply in a causal or other naturally law-like relation between the believer and the object of his belief. Armstrong suggests, quite plausibly, that 'When a true belief unsupported by reasons stands to the situation truly believed to exist as a thermometer reading in a good thermometer stands to the actual temperature, then we have non-inferential knowledge.'[1] McIver offers another route to the same general conclusion. He claims that the commonest use of the word 'know', in the third person, is:

> that which prompted Theaetetus' suggestion that 'knowledge' could be equated simply with 'true belief' ... The sentence in Tolstoy's *War and Peace*, 'Prince Andrew not only knew that he was going to die but knew that he was dying', takes it for granted

[1] Armstrong (1973) p. 166

that Prince Andrew was in fact dying and only makes the point
that his imminent death was (as it might not have been) envisaged
as such by the Prince himself. If Tolstoy had written 'Prince
Andrew thought that he was dying', the possibility would have
been left open that he might have been mistaken. But the choice
of the one word rather than the other would mark a difference
only in Tolstoy's representation of the circumstance, not in the
state of mind ascribed to Prince Andrew, the evidence he was
supposed to have, or anything like that.[1]

It looks as though what I know or am right in saying that you know
does not have to be something of whose truth anybody has assured
himself.

If you can know *p* without having consciously and deliberately
done anything to assure yourself that *p* is true, then that sort of
activity is also not necessary in order for you to know that you know
p. And if assurance of truth satisfies a want which knowing cannot
satisfy, knowing that one knows will be unable to satisfy it either.
This point is I think obscured by Armstrong. He analyses non-
inferential knowledge as true belief for which there are law-like
correlations between believer, proposition believed and what makes
this proposition true; and he analyses inferential knowledge in
terms of what non-inferential knowing causes us to believe. He
recognises that if this is what knowledge is, then we want another
mode of believing as well, but thinks that the additional want is
satisfied by knowing that one knows. 'We have certain beliefs', he
writes, 'Some correspond to the facts, some do not. Among those
which correspond to the facts, but are unsupported by reasons,
some have that empirical correlation with the facts of the sort which
has been described. All this may be granted . . . but how can we who
are, as it were, behind and locked up in our own belief, *determine*
which of our beliefs are properly correlated?'[2] His answer is that we
can know that we know, and knowledge that one knows is to be
analysed along the same lines as the first-order knowledge which
forms its object, i.e. in terms of true belief and law-like correlations.
But there is an obvious difference between on the one hand deter-
mining or assuring oneself that one's beliefs are true and involved in
certain law-like correlations, and on the other hand believing that

[1] McIver (1958) pp. 6–7
[2] Armstrong (1973) pp. 191–2 (my italics)

they are, even when one's belief that they are is itself true and involved in further law-like correlations. I would be just as anxious to determine whether I have a second-order knowledge analysed on the model of Armstrong's first-order knowledge as to determine whether I have this first-order knowledge itself. If thermometer-like knowledge is no substitute for assuring yourself of the truth then neither is thermometer-like knowledge that one knows.

To complete this section, I look at the relations between radical assurance and justified belief. In ordinary usage, to say that someone was justified in doing something, is to say that, partly at least because of what he himself thought about the relation between his action and some rule or principle or agreement, it was not a bad thing for him to do it. If we know that Arthur thought he had no right to resign, but still resigned, we will not say he was justified in resigning, even if we think that he had this right. And if we know that he thought he had a right to resign, and resigned, we may still say he was justified in doing so, even if we do not think that he had this right. Similarly, to say that someone is justified in believing something is to say that it is not a bad thing for him to believe it, and this partly at least because of what he believes about the way in which some general principle of evidence links p to the other propositions he believes, or about the way in which his believing p instantiates some general principle of investigation or consequential rationality. You can say that I am justified in believing that there is still coal in the cellar if you know that I inferred this from what I believe about the last delivery date and the number of sacks I usually get through in a week. You can say that I am justified in believing that no proposition is both true and false if I have somehow satisfied myself of its truth by what I take to be the right sort of non-evidence-adducing investigation. You can say that the old man not wanting to get upset is justified in believing his housekeeper is honest, even though he has done absolutely nothing to find out whether she really is (see pp. 8–9 above). This suggests that radical assurance is a species of what we would ordinarily call justified belief. Ordinary usage would also allow us to talk of being justified in being radically assured that p. This would mean that partly at least because of the activities by which you became radically assured that p, it was not a bad thing for you to have gained your radical assurance. And just as we may want to say that a man is by some standard justified in having a certain degree of partial belief, so we may also want to say that he is justified in having a certain degree of assurance, radical or otherwise (see p. 16 above).

Current philosophical usage is altogether more difficult to survey. And it is precisely because 'justified belief' and its cognates have already been the victims of so much conflicting and unilluminating stipulation that I decided to avoid introducing yet further technical senses of these terms and to couch my theses in terms of consequential rationality and assurance.

Lehrer's *Knowledge* is a good illustration of these tendencies. His book has been described as 'the definitive statement to date . . . of a subjective coherentist theory of justification'.[1] But it is nevertheless extremely difficult to find out what exactly he thinks a theory of justification is actually a theory of. Sometimes it seems that whether or not a man is justified in believing a proposition depends on the response he has actually made to someone's query or demand. This is the conception which Lehrer appeals to in some of his arguments against the thesis that, on pain of infinite regression or vicious circularity, some beliefs must be basic if any beliefs are to be justified at all. 'Justification,' he writes on p. 156, 'is ordinarily justification to someone else, and whether a justification given to someone suffices will depend on what that person is willing to grant.' And again, on p. 16, 'Justification need not proceed until all claims to knowledge employed in the justification are themselves justified. If we consider justification in a social context, the justification of knowledge claims need proceed only as long as some claim to knowledge is disputed. Thus, if we suppose that justification is a response to a query or demand, then there is no reason to suppose that the argument need proceed beyond the point at which agreement is reached. Hence, even if all completely justified beliefs are justified by evidence, not all claims to knowledge, employed to defend some other such claims, need themselves be justified.' But then, in the paragraph immediately following, Lehrer writes (my italics), 'any attempt to obtain a regress of justification could be met by arguing that some beliefs are completely justified because of the way they cohere with a system of beliefs rather than by appeal to evidence or *other form of argumentation*'. And it is precisely *p*'s coherence with a certain system of beliefs which, on Lehrer's final conclusion, is necessary and sufficient for *S* to be completely justified in believing *p*. *S* finds himself in that state, 'if and only if, within the corrected doxastic

[1] Pastin (1977) pp. 431, 6

system of S, p is believed to have a better chance of being true than the denial of p or any other statement that competes with p' (p. 198). And even when Lehrer is making S's justified belief that p a matter of p's relations to other propositions of the right kind, rather than of S's actual response to other people's objections, it is still not clear whether the propositions to which p must be related must actually be believed by S. On the p. 198 thesis, this may not be necessary, since S's corrected doxastic system is 'that subset of the doxastic system resulting when every statement is deleted which describes S as believing something he would cease to believe as an impartial and disinterested truth-seeker' (p. 190). But earlier on, in discussing the question of whether the incorrigibility of a belief is a sufficient condition for its being 'self-justified', Lehrer decides that it cannot be, on the grounds that if it were then you could be justified in believing the conjunction of an incorrigible proposition and a logical truth, no matter how foolish your reasons for believing the logical truth (pp. 84–5). This seems to show that whether you are justified in believing p depends on the reasons you actually have, i.e. on what else you actually believe, rather than just on the propositions which you would believe in certain hypothetical circumstances.

Even those writers on the 'theory of justification' who seem more consistent in their usage of 'justified belief' and its cognates rely often enough on the most partial and *ad hoc* stipulation, and do not trouble to show that the conditions they stipulate define a concept which we have some intelligible interest in being able to apply. Thus Cornman insists that an empirical statement p which is not 'self-justifying for s at t' is 'justified for s at t' only if there is a series of E-ancestors of p such that s is able to justify, individually, any statement in the series which is not self-justifying for s. It is not necessary that s *'actually'* justifies, individually, every statement in the series'.[1] x is an E-ancestor of p, he explains, '= df. there is an E-series, E, for p, such that for some set e_i in E, e_i would not justify $e_{i\text{-}i}$ if it did not contain x either as an element or as a conjunct of a statement that is logically equivalent to an element of e_i'.[2] E is an E-series for p '= df. E is a series of evidence sets, e_1 e_2, e_3, . . . such that: (1) e_1 justifies p; and (2) for any e_i in series E, e_i justifies $e_{i\text{-}i}$ in E'.[3] And x is self-justifying for s at t '= df. x is justified for s at t, and it is

---

[1] Cornman (1977) p. 290
[2] ibid. p. 288
[3] ibid.

false that it would be justified for s at t, only if it were to be justified by some relationship it has to some other statement or group of statements'.[1] But none of this tells us enough about what Cornman actually means by 'p is justified for s at t', for us to know whether we care about whether or not or how often his concept of justification is actually applicable. Does 'p is justified for s at t' entail 's believes p at t and p is at least probably true'? Cornman does not say, but the necessity of this condition is suggested by his insistence that 'a theory of justification is acceptable only if it does not yield that both a sentence and its denial are justified for the same person at the same time'.[2] But presumably other conditions are necessary as well. Should we perhaps add that there is something about the circumstances in which s believes p which makes it non-coincidental that p is at least probably true? Cornman gives us no hint. But it is clear at any rate that these two conditions are not sufficient, since he insists that when p is not self-justifying for s at t, p is not justified for s at t unless s himself has a certain ability, the ability to justify, individually, any non-self-justifying statement in a series of E-ancestors of p. This seems to mean that, for any non-self-justifying statement in the series, s is able to assure himself, by adducing evidence, that this statement is true, provided he does not also have to perform the same service for too many other statements in the series in too short a period of time. But Cornman does not explain why a concept of justification which requires this extra ability should be any more interesting, or for that matter any more appropriately called a concept of justification, than one determined simply by the first two conditions I mentioned, or one which also requires the believer to have the ability to justify *all* the statements in the series, or one which requires him actually to justify some or even all of the statements in the series. Given that we can actually distinguish these various concepts, it is surely better to have separate labels for those of them in whose applicability we have an intelligible interest, rather than simply to stamp the label 'justification' on to some apparently random agglomerate.

Similar objections apply I think to the initial stages of Pollock's powerful study of *Knowledge and Justification*. There is a difference, according to Pollock, between being justified in believing a proposition, and justifying a proposition.[3] To justify your belief that p, you

---

[1] ibid. p. 287   [2] ibid. p. 291
[3] Pollock (1974) pp. 25–7

must consciously appeal to some other proposition which you are justified in believing, i.e. evidentially, though perhaps not radically, assure yourself that p is true. But to be justified in believing that p, it is necessary and sufficient either that the belief that p is self-justifying, that simply having it is enough to make it justified, or that you hold some further justified belief which constitutes a good reason for believing that p. And although it may be necessary, in order for a non-self-justifying belief to be justified, that the believer is able to justify it, it is certainly not necessary that he has actually done so. Pollock then reaches various conclusions about being justified in believing a proposition, such as that you could not be justified in believing anything unless some beliefs were self-justifying and epistemologically basic. What he does not explain is what it actually means to be justified in believing something, and why justifying is less interesting than being justified.

Even Alston, in his subtle and lucid investigations of foundational theories of knowledge,[1] is curiously reticent about what, positively, he understands by 'N is justified in believing p'. He constantly emphasises a distinction between being justified in believing p and showing that p. Showing that p is for Alston an activity which involves the adducing of some other proposition q. Alston can find no reasons why we should want to show that p in a sense which requires anything more than that q is true, and constitutes adequate grounds for p, and that one is justified in believing q. And in particular he can find no reason why we should want to show that p in a sense which requires one also to be able to show that this additional proposition q is true.[2] The ability to show that p is in my terminology the ability to gain a species of non-radical evidential assurance. But what is it to be justified in believing p? There is I think an unresolved tension in the little Alston does say about this. On the one hand he seems to suggest that some true beliefs may be only mediately as opposed to immediately justified, i.e. are only justified by something which 'includes the believer's possessing certain other justified beliefs'.[3] On the other hand it is also a 'live possibility' that some immediately justified beliefs are justified by the fact that makes them true.[4] But if being true really is sufficient for immediate justification no true belief will be mediately justified only.

[1] Alston (1976a and b)   [2] Alston (1976a) pp. 176–9
[3] Alston (1976b) p. 289
[4] ibid. p. 295

Later on, I shall need to look in a more detailed way at some of the actual arguments about justificatory regression, justification by experience, self-justifying beliefs, and so on which these and other writers have put forward. But I postpone further discussion of current theories of justification until I come on to develop my own theses about the scarcity and desirability of radical assurance.

If we ignore all current technical senses, and allow 'justified belief' its pristine indeterminacy, then this diagram illustrates the relations between radical assurance and the various other species of justified belief which I have so far distinguished.

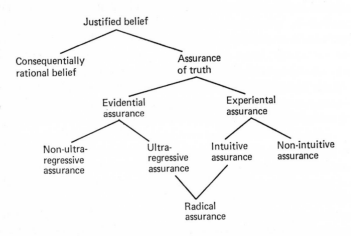

(5) *Self-evidence and intuitive assurance*

You have intuitively assured yourself that *p*, in the definition of section (2), if you have experientially assured yourself that *p* and the experience which terminates your conscious and deliberate activity of investigation is merely that of acquiring a powerful conviction of *p*'s truth (see p. 20 above). And as I said, the claim that there are true propositions with respect to which we can have an experience of that kind, and such that there is a non-coincidental link between our having such an experience and the fact that in believing them we are believing the truth, is one version of the traditional rationalist claim that there are self-evident propositions or propositions which we can metaphorically see to be true. Another interpretation of what it is to 'see' that *p* would postulate, not inner-sensory experience whose intentional object is the acquiring of the belief that *p*, but non-sensory experience with an outer and possibly abstract intentional object, non-sensory experience whose intentional object is somehow what makes *p* true.[1] Gödel toyed with an interpretation of this second kind in his account of mathematical intuition: 'despite their remoteness from sense experience, we do have something like a perception also of the objects of set theory, as is seen from the fact that the axioms force themselves upon us as being true. I don't see any reason why we should have less confidence in this kind of perception, i.e. in mathematical intuition, than in sense-perception. That something besides the sensations actually is immediately given follows (independently of mathematics) from the fact that even our ideas referring to physical objects contain constituents qualitatively different from sensations or mere combinations of sensations, e.g. the idea of the object itself . . . It by no means follows . . . that the data of this second kind, because they cannot be associated with actions of certain things upon our sense organs, are purely subjective, as Kant asserted. Rather, they, too, may represent an aspect of objective reality, but, as opposed to the sensations, their presence in us may be due to another kind of relationship between ourselves and reality'.[2] Both interpretations are I think compatible with the thesis that metaphorical seeing is a phenomenologically unique experience, and perhaps even with the thesis, recently advanced by Pollock, that there are phenomenologically distinct kinds of metaphorical seeing, whose differences correspond to whether what is 'seen' is a truth, an implication, or a possibility.[3] But whether or not there really is such a thing as non-coincidentally veridical and non-sensory experience whose intentional object is outer and abstract, it is metaphorical seeing of the other kind which radical and non-evidential assurance requires. When non-evidential, radical assurance requires an activity of investigation which terminates in a non-coincidentally veridical experience whose intentional object is the acquiring of a belief. For, as I stipulated in the previous section, radical assurance requires consciousness of the nature of the activity of investigation by means of which the assurance is reached. And, as we saw in section (2), all non-evidential assurance is experiential and consciousness of the nature of the activity by means of which you have gained experiential assurance is incompatible with the continued existence of an originally non-intuitive experiential assurance (see p. 20 above).

[1] For explanations of this terminology see pp. 19–20 above
[2] Gödel (1964) pp. 271–2   [3] Pollock (1974) pp. 321–3

Suppose for example that I assure myself that no proposition is both true and false by an activity which terminates in a non-intuitive non-sensory experience, an experience whose intentional object is somehow what makes it true that no proposition is both true and false. Then in being conscious of the nature of my activity I must either think that the proposition that I had this experience is evidence for the truth of the proposition which my activity assured me of, which transmutes my assurance into the evidential mode, or think that the proposition that I had this experience is no evidence at all, which abolished my assurance altogether (see p. 22 above). If on the other hand my activity terminates in an experience which is merely the experience of acquiring the conviction that no proposition is both true and false, then I can be conscious that this is how it has terminated without in the least thinking that the proposition that this is how it has terminated is evidence for the truth of what the activity assured me of. Propositions of the form 'N had an experience whose intentional object was that p' are, if intelligible at all, evidence for p. Propositions of the form 'N had an experience whose intentional object was his acquiring of the belief that p' are not evidence for p.

And yet, even if there is metaphorical seeing of the sort which radical and non-evidential assurance requires – the experience of acquiring, by means other than sensory experience or the adducing of evidence, an especially powerful and non-coincidentally veridical conviction – it is still very far from clear what the activity of investigation which terminates in this metaphorical seeing could possibly consist in. When experiential assurance terminates in literal seeing, the activity is deciding to go and see, and then taking the necessary physical steps. Is the analogue of deciding to go and see deciding to put yourself in the position to gain an especially powerful conviction? If so, what activity is there, analogous to taking up a suitable viewpoint, yet not actually involving the consideration of possible evidence? Maybe the activity of investigation which terminates in metaphorical vision is an activity of thinking about real or imaginary instances or analogies. You grasp the truth of the general proposition that no proposition is both true and false by reflecting on such propositions as that the earth is both round and not round.[1] But then why exactly is your reflexion not an adducing of evidence?

[1] Cf. Chisholm (1977) pp. 38–40

But I am less interested in pursuing these doubts than in convincing you that even if there were such a thing as radical and intuitive assurance, radical assurance would still be something we cannot often obtain. The first step is to set out some plausibly modest assumptions about the scope of radical and intuitive assurance. Then in the next chapter I will argue that the scope of radical assurance is entirely dependent on the scope of radical and intuitive assurance, and explore the further possibility that these plausible assumptions, though too modest to allow us much radical assurance, are not too modest to prevent us from being radically assured that there is this relation of dependence, if all assurance is either experiential or evidential.

If a self-evident proposition is now defined as one which at least one averagely endowed person can on my favoured interpretation metaphorically see to be true, a proposition will be one of whose truth we can gain radical and intuitive assurance only if it is self-evident. So the assumptions which seem to me plausible can be set out as assumptions about which propositions are in this technical sense self-evident. They are as follows. (1) A proposition is self-evident only if it does not entail the existence of any spatio-temporally or temporally located entity other than a single subject of consciousness. (2) A proposition is self-evident only if it does not entail that someone is in a particular mental state or possesses a particular mental power other than the state or power of being conscious. If the proposition that I exist does not entail that anyone else does, then perhaps (1) allows it to be self-evident, and allows more particularly that I myself can 'see' it to be true. Similarly, (1) may allow you to 'see' that you exist. But the proposition that we both exist is not self-evident, according to (1), since it entails the existence of more than one temporally or spatio-temporally located entity. Neither you nor I can 'see' it to be true. (2) prevents us from ascribing self-evidence to propositions of such forms as '*N* wants *x*', '*N* does not want *x*', '*N* sees *x*', '*N* does not see *x*', '*N* believes *p*', '*N* does not believe *p*', '*p* is self-evident', '*p* is not self-evident'. Neither (1) nor (2) prevents us from ascribing self-evidence to such propositions as 'if anything is red then it is extended' or 'the proposition that it looks red is evidence for the proposition that it is red', which either do not entail the existence of anything, or do not entail the existence of anything temporally or spatio-temporally located.

Underlying these two assumptions is the further and I think

equally plausible assumption that if there is indeed such a thing as metaphorical seeing, however interpreted, then if one can 'see' that *p* one cannot also have inner or outer sensory experience that *p*. Just because one can have outer sensory experience that there is a dandelion in the field, and inner sensory experience that one believes that there is, or that one is thinking that there is, one cannot also 'see' that there is, or that one believes or thinks that there is. It may help to consider a parallel assumption about a priori knowledge. Some propositions knowable a posteriori are also knowable a priori (e.g. mathematical truths which can be either 'seen' or known by inference from propositions about the reputation of someone who tells you they are true). But no propositions non-inferentially knowable a posteriori are also non-inferentially knowable a priori. If that much seems plausible, you now need only to reflect that in knowing that *p* both a priori and non-inferentially you are metaphorically seeing that *p*, and that if non-inferential knowledge that *p* is a posteriori rather than a priori when it is gained simply by sensory experience that *p*, 'sensory experience' will presumably include the operations of inner as well as outer sense. (1) and (2) have provisos about the subject of consciousness and the state or power of being conscious because it is not clear that one can indeed have inner sensory experience of oneself as a subject of consciousness: it is not clear that when one's awareness of believing that there is a dandelion in a field is accompanied by an awareness of oneself as the subject of that awareness of believing, both awarenesses are inner-sensory experiences.

If, contrary to (2), '*p* is self-evident' seems the form of a proposition which is itself self-evident, then I repeat that in asserting a proposition of this form you are claiming something about what mental powers an averagely endowed person happens to possess. From the fact that *p*'s truth is graspable without either sensory experience or the citation of evidence it does not follow that the same is also true of this fact about how *p*'s truth is graspable.

Self-evidence needs also to be distinguished from incorrigibility. By '*p* is incorrigible for *N*', I mean that necessarily, if *N* believes *p*, then *p*. It may then be, though actually I doubt it, that there are incorrigible propositions among those whose self-evidence is excluded by (1) and (2).[1] But certainly incorrigibility in no way guarantees self-evidence. The most that you are empowered to do

[1] See Lehrer (1974) pp. 80–100

by the fact that *p* is incorrigible for you is to cite, as evidence for *p*, a proposition which you can often affirm with some confidence, namely the proposition that *p* is something you believe. Whereas if *p* is self-evident you can know its truth without any citation of evidence at all.

What are the relations between self-evidence and necessary truth? This deserves something better than a direct answer. For it is far from clear why we are obliged to postulate the existence of necessary truths at all, and far from clear that 'necessary truth' can be understood except as a name of an explanatory postulate. One argument for saying that there are true propositions of the form 'All *A*s must be *B*s' is that the laws of natural science need to be of this form if they are to be distinguishable, as obviously they are distinguishable, from mere true spatio-temporally unrestricted generalisations. They are distinguishable only by the fact that they support counter-factual conditionals. And we can explain what it is for them to support counter-factual conditionals only by supposing that they are of the form 'All *A*s must be *B*s'. The argument can be met by regarding the expression of a counter-factual as the condensation of an argument. If I say 'If *x* were an *A* it would be a *B*', I am recapitulating and condensing the following argument: 'Suppose *x* is an *A*; all *A*s are *B*s; so *x* is a *B*'. And if I say that a law of nature to the effect that all *A*s are *B*s supports the counter-factual conditional 'If *x* were an *A* it would be a *B*', then all I mean is that there is good inductive evidence for the 'All *A*s are *B*s' premiss in the argument which is condensed in the counter-factual.[1] Is there any reason for believing in the existence of true propositions of the form 'All *A*s must, logically or conceptually, be *B*s' other than the thought that there are generalisations like 'No proposition is both true and false' and 'Everything red is coloured' which could not support counter-factual conditionals unless they were about logical or conceptual necessities? If not, why cannot this thought be disposed of in exactly the same way as the counter-factual conditional argument for taking laws of natural science as propositions about objective necessities in nature? To say 'If anything were a proposition, it could not be both true and false' would be to condense and recapitulate an argument with at least one self-evident premiss. We could continue to think of ourselves as having knowledge of the proposition that no proposition is both true and false and perhaps also as

[1] See Mackie (1973) pp. 114–19

being psychologically unable to conceive its negation and hence to revise it, but we would not need to postulate superfluous mysteries about objective necessity.

But it would be irrelevant to my present purposes to pursue these doubts. Assuming as I shall now do that there are necessary truths, some but not all propositions are necessarily true which plausible assumptions allow to be self-evident, and all sufficiently complicated necessary truths are non-self-evident. 'I exist' will be a contingency which plausible assumptions allow to be self-evident; 'If any two men either love each other or hate each other then either there is a man who loves all men, or for every man there is some man whom he hates', a necessary truth which we need some evidence to grasp.

As I said, a proposition must be self-evident if it is to be one of whose truth we can gain radical and intuitive assurance. But not all radical assurance is intuitive, and it is not even immediately clear that non-intuitive radical assurance depends on the intuitive kind. In arguing that there is this dependence I shall use a distinction between two kinds of radical assurance, one of which has this dependence by definition. I will say that you are α-assured that p if and only if you are radically and evidentially assured that p but not just by being β-assured that p, and that you are β-assured that p if and only if you are radically assured that p and either (a) you are intuitively assured that p or (b) you are evidentially assured that p and there is a proposition of whose truth you are intuitively assured and which you believe to be overriding evidence either for p, or for a proposition which you believe to be overriding evidence for p, or for a proposition which you believe to be overriding evidence for a proposition which you believe to be overriding evidence for p, or ..., and so on. If, as I argued earlier (see pp. 34–5 above) all radical assurance is either evidential or intuitive, then, given the ultra-regressiveness of radical and evidential assurance (see pp. 32–4 above), it is also true that all radical assurance is either α-assurance or β-assurance. And if, as I shall argue in the next chapter, this makes α-assurance impossible, then radical and β-assurance have a co-extensive scope, and the scope of radical assurance is ultimately dependent on the scope of self-evidence. In traditional rationalist philosophy, there is a distinction between propositions just 'seen' to be true and propositions derivable from those simply 'seen' to be true by steps whose validity is simply 'seen'. There is a parallel division between two kinds of propositions which we can β-assure ourselves to be true. On the one hand there are propositions which we can radically and intuitively assure ourselves to be true, and which are therefore self-evident in the sense that we can experience our acquisition of an especially powerful and non-coincidentally veridical conviction of their truth. On the other hand there are propositions which, though not self-evident and therefore not ones which we can radically and intuitively assure ourselves to be true, are nevertheless ones of whose truth we can gain β-assurance of the evidential kind. No rationalist succeeded in deriving much of a belief-system from the simply 'seen' by steps of simply 'seeable' validity. Nor, it seems, is there much that we can be β-assured of, if my initial assumptions about self-evidence are true. Nor, therefore, does there seem to be much that we can be radically assured of, if my initial assumptions about self-evidence are true, and radical and β-assurance have a co-extensive scope.

2

The limits of radical assurance

All assurance is either evidential or experiential. So all radical assurance is either evidential or intuitive. So all radical assurance is either α-assurance or β-assurance. So radical and β-assurance have a co-extensive scope if either α-assurance is impossible or every proposition of whose truth you can be α-assured is one of whose truth you can be β-assured. It is this last disjunction about α-assurance which I chiefly want to consider in the present chapter. If the disjunction is true, and radical and β-assurance do therefore have a co-extensive scope, then on plausible assumptions about self-evidence it is hard to see that we can gain much radical assurance. And if it is also true, as I shall argue in chapters 3 and 4, that extensive radical assurance, or an extensive power to gain it, is something we are nevertheless liable to want, then a sceptical doctrine seems to follow, and a sceptical doctrine which does not just reduce to the complaint that some arbitrarily demanding cognitive concept is hardly ever applicable. Conceivably, the whole plan is over-elaborate. Maybe the active element in any form of assurance allows us to construct a simpler and more sweeping deterministic scepticism, which requires no proof that radical assurance is something we are liable to want in vain. I will try to dispose of this possibility in the first section of the chapter before turning in section (2) to the disjunction about α-assurance.

(1) *Determinism*

If '*N* is justified in believing *p*' entails '*N* has performed a free mental action' then 'There are no free actions' entails that there are no propositions which *N* is justified in believing. This thought has often been seized on by believers in free action: if there are no propositions which you are justified in believing then neither are you justified in believing that there are no free actions. One might on the other hand be inclined to argue that just because there are no free actions, there is nothing that you are justified in believing. The coherence of the concept of free action might seem more doubtful than the existence of justified belief. To many philosophers it has seemed necessarily true that free actions are caused (because 'not random'), but also necessarily true that free actions are not caused (because in the circumstances of their performance it was possible for their agent not to have performed them). If the concept of free action is itself incoherent, then the libertarian involvements of justified believing show not so much that there is a special problem about being justified in believing that there are no free actions, but rather that there is a general problem about being justified in believing anything at all. Does justified believing really require free action on the believer's part? If 'N is justified in believing p' means 'N has assured himself that p is true', then it is not too implausible to suppose that it does. Certainly you need conscious and deliberate activity to assure yourself that a proposition is true.

The argument could be strengthened a little. We could allow that it may after all be logically possible for uncaused free actions to exist, and insist only that caused free actions are both necessarily non-existent and required for the assurance of truth. We could insist more particularly that while assuring yourself that a proposition is true requires you freely to perform an action you want to perform, a free action which the agent wanted to perform cannot but be caused by his wanting to perform it, and a caused action cannot be free. I shall now look rapidly at some of the obstacles which stand in the way of even this strengthened argument for the non-existence of assurance of truth.

Opponents of anti-determinist applications of the supposed connexion between justified believing and free action on the believer's part have often stressed that knowledge, so far from requiring free action on the believer's part, in fact requires his subjection to the world, and the causation of his believing by what makes the object of his believing true. Wiggins goes so far as to suggest that this subjection may even be a condition for the existence of anything properly describable as belief:

> unless I am God or Reality itself – unless my knowledge is not human knowledge at all – reality is most of it precisely what is independent of me and my will. Its arrangement is precisely what is *not* up to me ... if my beliefs are to relate to the world at all, I

simply have to lay myself open to the world in order to let the
phenomena put their print upon me. How otherwise can my
beliefs even aim at a correct account of the world? If my state is
one which seals itself off from the outside, this surely enfeebles its
claim to be a state of *belief*. For there is subtracted everything which
distinguishes belief from fantasy and the state of the sane man who
can tell the difference of belief and fantasy from the state of the
lunatic who by his own inability to distinguish them approaches
the point where he can hardly be credited with belief at all.[1]

May not these considerations tell also against the sceptical argument
we are now considering? Radical assurance requires a non-coincidental relation between one's activity of gaining assurance about *p*
and the fact that in believing *p* one is believing the truth (see p.
34 above). Surely that much at least is required by any non-subject-
ive concept of assurance, radical or otherwise, which we actually
want to apply? And how can coincidence be excluded unless we
postulate a causal relation?

One could answer, ad hominem, that there is room for both causal
relations and activity. As I suggested when defining radical assurance, the activity of investigating a proposition's truth-value might
consist in putting yourself into a position in which you are caused
to believe the proposition by what makes it true (see p. 34 above).
Or, equally ad hominem, one might ask how there can be the causal
relations necessary to exclude coincidence when the proposition we
believe is about the future, or is a proposition to the effect that some
other proposition is probably true. But really the whole line of
objection is misconceived. Our sceptic claims that you cannot assure
yourself of a proposition's truth without acting freely. Suppose we
go so far as to insist that the condition of non-coincidence cannot be
satisfied unless the actual activity of investigation is caused. Why
should that threaten the sceptic? He insists himself that the activity
of investigation must be caused. His whole argument is that the
causation of the activity is both necessary and impossible. The
objection, if there is anything in it, can only reinforce the argument.
The sceptic thinks that the activity of investigation necessary for
assuring yourself of truth must be caused by the investigator's
wanting to perform it. The objection is only that it may need to
have another cause as well.

[1] Wiggins (1970) p. 143

Let me turn back now to the original sceptical argument, unforti-fied by the unsuccessful objection. The argument was that assurance requires activity which is caused because wanted but uncaused because free. Why should it be supposed that when a man does what he wants to do, the wanting causes his action? The sceptic's answer is that there is clearly some sort of explanatory relation between the wanting and the action, and no reason to think that the relation is anything but causal. You could object that since actions actually consist in movements caused by wantings and believings, wanting could only cause action if, absurdly, a sequence of events could be caused by one of its own components. But if the wanting that causes an action is a wanting of that action, and if wanting is also a necessary component of action, then the component wanting must, on pain of infinite regression, be a wanting not of the action itself, but of the movement which is the action's other component. Nor does it seem possible to extract any relevant truth from the hazy objection that while causes must be logically distinct from their effects, wanting of actions can be identified only by reference to the actions by which they are satisfied.

Things become more difficult for the sceptic when we ask why it is supposed to be impossible that an action should be both caused and free. The strongest argument for this impossibility is I think as follows:

(1) If N did x in circumstances C and did it freely, then he could, in C, have refrained from doing x

(2) If N did x in circumstances C and did it freely, then in C it was physically and psychologically possible for him to have refrained from doing x (from (1))

(3) If N did x in circumstances C and did it freely, then there are no nomological propositions whose conjunction with 'cir-cumstances like C obtained' entails 'an event like N's doing x occurred'   (from (2))

(4) If N did x in circumstances C and was caused to do it by a part of C then there are nomological propositions to the effect that whenever there are circumstances like C there is an event like N's doing x

(5) If N did x in circumstances C and did it freely then he was not caused to do it by a part of C (from (3) and (4))

Resistance can take many forms. You might try to show that we can

content ourselves with a concept of freedom which makes (1) false. Maybe we do not mind not having the ability, in one and the same set of circumstances, either to do something or not to do it. Maybe the only sort of freedom we really care about consists simply in doing what we want, or doing what we want when the want in question is not one which we do not want to have. Or, better, you might try to show that we have no reason to apply any concept of causality to actions, other than one which allows us to say that if there are indeed nomological propositions whose conjunction with 'circumstances like C obtained' entails 'an event like N's doing x occurred' then this is only because N did not exercise his power in C to refrain from doing x. Relative to that concept of causality, either (1) will not entail (2) or (2) will not entail (3).

But let us suppose that the sceptic about assurance really is entitled to say that there are no free actions which the agent wanted to perform. He still has to convince us that 'N has assured himself that p' entails 'N freely did something which he wanted to do'. He might suggest that investigation requires deliberation. You wonder whether to take this or that objection seriously, to look at this or that side of the problem first, and so on. And you cannot deliberate about whether or not to do something without believing that there is more than one thing which you are free to do. Equally, actions which issue out of deliberation and conform to the conclusion reached in this deliberation will presumably be ones which the agent wanted to perform. But this is still not enough. It shows only that 'N has assured himself that p' entails 'N performed an action which he wanted to perform and which he believed, before performing, that he was free to perform'. And the most we can get by conjoining this conditional with the thesis that there are no free actions which the agent wanted to perform is that 'N has assured himself that p' entails that at one stage in the process of gaining assurance N believed something which was false. The conclusion is not even faintly paradoxical. To advance any further, the sceptic must somehow obliterate the distinction between action and free action. Perhaps he can show that all actions are either volitions or have volitions as components, and then argue for the senselessness of supposing that volitions are ever unfree. That looks like a hazardous line of thought, and anyway there are uncertainties enough in the earlier stages of his argument. The same difficulties remain if he brings in the additional point that any assurance worth the name requires a non-coincidental relation between the activity of gaining assurance and the fact that in believing what you are assured of you are believing the truth. Maybe the relation cannot be non-coincidental without the activity's being caused. But how do we show that the activity must also be free, and not just activity which the agent antecedently believed free? I turn then to the special problems of radical assurance, and more particularly to the disjunction about a-assurance whose truth gives radical and β-assurance a co-extensive scope.

(2) *A disjunction about a-assurance*

The disjunction we now have to consider is that either a-assurance is impossible, or every proposition of whose truth you can be a-assured is one of whose truth you can be β-assured. It will be a help, in considering this disjunction, if I repeat some of my previous definitions. You are a-assured that *p* if and only if you are radically and evidentially assured that *p* but not just by being β-assured that *p*, and you are β-assured that *p* if and only if you are radically assured that *p* and either (a) you are intuitively assured that *p* or (b) you are evidentially assured that *p* and there is a proposition of whose truth you are intuitively assured and which you believe either to be overriding evidence for *p*, or for a proposition which you believe to be overriding evidence for *p*, or for a proposition which you believe to be overriding evidence for a proposition which you believe to be overriding evidence for *p*, or . . ., and so on. You are radically assured that *p* if and only if (i) you have assured yourself that *p*; (ii) *p* is true; (iii) if your assurance that *p* is evidential then it is ultra-regressive; (iv) on gaining your assurance that *p*, you are conscious of the nature of the activity of investigation by means of which your assurance has been gained; (v) there is a non-coincidental relation between your activity of gaining assurance that *p* and the fact that in believing *p* you are believing what is true; and (vi) if your assurance that *p* is evidential then conditions (i)–(v) would still hold if we substituted for *p* any of those additional propositions whose truth you must be assured of in order for condition (iii) to be satisfied.

There are two features of radical assurance in general which are especially relevant to the possibility of a-assurance. One is that evidential radical assurance is ultra-regressive. The relevant part of what that means is that if you are radically and evidentially assured that p, then you are assured of the truth of the proposition q which you affirm to be evidence for p, and if evidentially assured of the truth of q then also assured of the truth of the proposition q_1 which you affirm to be evidence for q, and so on indefinitely (see pp. 32–4). The other relevant general feature of radical assurance is that if you are radically and evidentially assured that p then you are also radically assured of the truth of any proposition of whose truth you must be assured in order for the requirement of the ultra-regressiveness of radical evidential assurance to be satisfied. (Suppose that you are radically and evidentially assured that p and so, by (iii), assured of the truth of the proposition q which you affirm to be evidence for p. By (vi), (i)–(v) still hold when this proposition q is substituted for p in (i)–(v). So if (vi) holds true as well when q is substituted for p in (vi), then you are radically assured that p. But (vi) does still hold when q is substituted for p in (vi), because the propositions of whose truth you have to be assured in order for (iii) to be satisfied when q is substituted for p in (iii) are a subset of the propositions of whose truth you have to be assured in order for the original (iii) to be satisfied.)

Let us now look more closely at a-assurance, in the light of these two features of radical and evidential assurance. You are a-assured that p only if you are radically and evidentially assured that p. So if you are a-assured that p, then, by the two features just noted, there is a proposition q of whose truth you are radically assured and which you affirm to be evidence for p. It is, however, a necessary condition for you to be a-assured that p, that you are not radically assured that p just by being β-assured that p. And it is a sufficient condition for your being β-assured that p that you are radically and evidentially assured that p and intuitively assured of the truth of the proposition q which you affirm to be evidence for p. So if you are a-assured that p then the proposition q which you affirm to be evidence for p is one of whose truth you are not merely radically, but also non-intuitively assured. But all radical assurance is either evidential or intuitive. So you are evidentially assured that q. But this means that there is a proposition q_1 of whose truth you are radically assured and which you affirm to be evidence for q. And by the same argument you are evidentially assured that q_1, and there is a proposition q_2 of whose truth you are radically assured and which you affirm to be evidence for q_1. And so on. Does the inescapability of this infinite regress make a-assured believing impossible?

'Infinite justificatory regression' is sometimes thought to be made impossible by the fact that no one can believe an infinite number of different propositions simultaneously. Certainly there can be no two identical propositions in the infinite series of propositions p, q, q_1, q_2, ... which figures in the regress of assurance required for you to be a-assured that p. No proposition in the series can be identical to its immediate successor in the series. If it were, then, by the irreflexiveness of the relation 'is evidence for', its immediate successor would not be evidence for it (see p. 27 above). And this means that it would not be a proposition of whose truth you were radically and evidentially assured. For that requires you to be radically assured that what you affirm to be evidence *is* evidence. And you cannot be *radically* assured that it is evidence unless it is true that it is evidence. Nor can any proposition in the series be identical to a proposition which succeeds it but is not its immediate successor. For this would violate the asymmetricality of the relation between being evidentially assured that p and being evidentially assured that q, when you are evidentially assured that p by adducing q as evidence either for p or for a proposition which you adduce as evidence for p, or . . ., etc. (see p. 29 above). You cannot for example be at one and the same time evidentially assured that p by adducing q as evidence for p, evidentially assured that q by adducing q_1 as evidence for q, and evidentially assured that q_1 by adducing p as evidence for q_1. For then you would be evidentially assured that p by adducing q_1 as evidence for a proposition which you adduced as evidence for p, and at the same time evidentially assured that q_1 by adducing p as evidence for q_1. And yet, is it really clear that you must simultaneously believe every proposition which having a-assurance requires you to believe? Why is it impossible for someone to become radically and evidentially assured that p by affirming other propositions whose truth he was at one time radically assured of, but which he no longer believes when he comes to believe p? And is it clear anyway that you cannot simultaneously believe an infinite number of propositions? Maybe someone who believes some proposition about an infinite set believes an infinite number of propositions each of which concerns a different element of the set.

Does a-assurance require the impossible feat of performing, in a finite time, an infinite number of tasks of finite and more or less equal duration? Suppose a man is a-assured that p. He will need to have considered what might be evidence for p, which will have taken a little time, and then, since he has to be evidentially assured of the truth of the proposition q which he affirms to be evidence for p, he will need to have considered what might be evidence for q, which will have taken a little more time, and so on ad infinitum. This argument against α-assurance also leaves me with a certain unease. Why is it impossible for the man somehow to grasp all at once that each proposition in the series p, q, q_1, ... has a successor which is evidence for it?

But even if one or other of these temporal or psychological arguments against α-assurance is sound we shall also want to know whether or not my initial assumptions about self-evidence allow you to be β-assured that if all radical assurance is either α- or β-assurance then α-assurance is impossible, or at any rate that if all radical assurance is either α- or β-assurance then you cannot α-assure yourself of anything which you cannot also β-assure yourself of. And clearly that is not a goal which these temporal and psychological arguments will allow us to reach. For they rely on premisses for which, on my initial assumptions about self-evidence, we cannot gain β-assurance (see p. 45 above). These assumptions do not allow us to be β-assured that it is impossible simultaneously to believe an infinite number of propositions. And even if they allow us to be β-assured that α-assurance would require the completion of an infinite number of separate investigatory tasks, they do not allow us to be β-assured that only a finite time is available for their completion, or even that they could not be completed in a finite time. Suppose it took our man less time to consider whether q_1 was evidence for q than to consider whether q was evidence for p, less time to consider whether q_2 was evidence for q_1 than to consider whether q_1 was evidence for q and so on ad infinitum. Unless there was some minimum time it took him to consider whether any proposition was evidence for another, then he could consider each of an infinite number of evidential relations in a finite time, just as he could, in a finite time, perform the infinite number of actions which constitute traversing the infinite number of smaller and smaller intervals involved in running a mile.[1] On my initial assumptions about self-evidence, we cannot be β-assured that there is any such minimum time.

It is sometimes thought that if there is any proposition which you are justified or reasonable in believing, then there is some proposition

[1] Grünbaum (1968), pp. 90 ff; cf. Peirce (1960), pp. 154–5

which you are justified or reasonable in believing irrespective of whether you believe any proposition which is a reason or support for it, and furthermore that we can demonstrate this thesis merely by pointing out that if it were indeed a sufficient condition for a man to be reasonable or justified in believing p that he believed a proposition q which was a reason or support for p, believed a proposition q_1 which was a reason or support for q, and so on ad infinitum, then he could be reasonable or justified in believing anything at all, however fantastic or obviously absurd. Thus Deutscher, aiming to show that you cannot be reasonable in believing anything, unless you are reasonable in believing a proposition by virtue of something other than believing another proposition which is a reason for it, asks us to consider by contrast the following conditions for a man to hold reasonable belief. (i) He is reasonable in holding a belief only if he holds it for a reason or reasons; (ii) he has a reason R for a belief A only if he believes that R; (iii) he is reasonable in believing A because of the reason R only if he reasonably believes that R; (iv) no belief is a reason for itself. 'It follows from these conditions', Deutscher says,

> that he can be reasonable in holding one belief only if he holds an infinity of others. Suppose he did have an infinite set of beliefs, however absurd this may appear; is it impossible that he should hold none of these beliefs for any real reason? Couldn't it be one vast delusion system? Is a man reasonable in holding one belief merely because he holds another whose propositional content is suitably related to the second, and so on? Might not a man just dream up a system and be ingenious enough always to extend his story in a logical fashion? How can the mere continuous extension of a belief system guarantee the rationality of the members of the system?[1]

There is another argument of the same kind in Pollock's *Knowledge and Justification*, designed to show that if anyone is justified in believing anything, he must have an 'epistemologically basic' belief, or belief which he is justified in holding without being able to justify it on the basis of any other belief. We are to consider what would follow if it were a sufficient condition for a man to be justified in holding a belief that P that 'he holds an infinite (possible circular) sequence of beliefs $Q_1 \, Q_2, \ldots$ such that P is supported by some of

[1] Deutscher (1973) pp. 5–6

the beliefs in the sequence and each belief in turn is supported by later beliefs in the sequence'. If this condition were sufficient, a man 'could be justified in believing P if he also happened to believe each of

$$Q_1, Q_1 \supset P; Q_2, Q_2 \supset Q_1,$$
$$Q_2 \supset (Q_1 \supset P) \; Q_3, Q_3 \supset Q_2,$$
$$Q_3 \supset (Q_2 \supset Q_1), Q_3 \supset [Q_2 \supset (Q_1 \supset P)],$$
$$Q_4, Q_4 \supset Q_3, Q_4 \supset (Q_3 \supset Q_2),$$
$$Q_4 \supset [Q_3 \supset (Q_2 \supset Q_1)],$$
$$Q_4 \supset \{Q_3 \supset [Q_2 \supset (Q_1 \supset P)]\},$$
$$Q_5, \ldots$$

In this sequence of beliefs, each belief is supported by beliefs later in the sequence, but the beliefs are nowhere tied down in any way to the evidence of S's senses. As long as a person's beliefs form such a coherent set, he could hold any beliefs at all regarding the colours, shapes, sizes, etc., of things, regardless of how they look or feel to him.' He could be justified in believing that all of his senses mislead in a systematic way. But this is manifestly absurd. 'It is impossible for a person to be justified in believing that *all* of his senses systematically mislead him *all* of the time.'[1]

If these arguments of Deutscher and Pollock are sound, then we should be able to use their underlying idea in order to show that a-assurance is impossible. For necessarily, if you are a-assured that p, there does not have to be a proposition of whose truth you are non-evidentially assured, and which you affirm to be evidence for p, or for a proposition which you affirm to be evidence for p, or, etc.

But both arguments are defective. Let us say that you are propositionally reasonable in believing a proposition if it is a necessary condition for you to be reasonable in believing that proposition that you are reasonable in believing some proposition which is your reason for believing it. In these terms, Deutscher aims to show that

(A) If N is propositionally reasonable in believing p then there is some proposition which he is non-propositionally reasonable in believing

He thinks that if you deny (A) you are committed to

[1] Pollock (1974) pp. 27–8

(B) It is a sufficient condition for N to be reasonable in believing p, that q is his reason for believing p, q_1 his reason for believing q, and so on ad infinitum

And (B) is absurd because

(C) It is possible that q is N's reason for believing p, q_1 his reason for believing q, and so on ad infinitum, where p, q, q_1 ... form a vast delusion system

This can be refuted as follows. Either (i) 'N is reasonable in believing p' entails 'p is at least probably true' and 'q is N's reason for believing p' entails 'q is true', or (ii) one of these entailments holds but the other does not, or (iii) neither entailment holds. If (i) then (C) is false, and so (B) cannot be reduced to absurdity by being conjoined with (C). If (ii) then it is not clear why a man who denies (A) should be committed to (B) in the first place. If (iii) then maybe (C) is true, but it is not clear why any absurdity should follow from its conjunction with (B).

Pollock's argument has a similar defect. He aims to show that

(A1) If N is justified in believing a proposition only because he has a reason for believing it, then there is some epistemologically basic proposition which he believes

By denying (A1) you are supposedly committed to

(B1) It is a sufficient condition for being justified in believing p that you believe an infinite sequence of propositions q_1, q_2, q_3, ... such that p is supported by some of the propositions in the sequence and each proposition is supported by later propositions in the sequence

And (B1) is absurd because

(C1) It is possible that N believes p, q_1, $q_1 \supset p$, q_2, $q_2 \supset q_1$, etc. where p is the proposition that all of N's senses systematically mislead him all of the time

But either (i) 'N is justified in believing p' entails 'p is at least probably true' and 'q supports p' entails 'q is true', or (ii) one of these entailments holds but the other does not, or (iii) neither entailment holds. (i) can be eliminated since in Pollock's account it is a sufficient condition for one proposition to support another that it materially implies it. If (ii) then it is not clear why someone who denies (A1) should be committed to (B1) in the first place. If (iii) then maybe (C1) is true, but it is not clear why any absurdity should follow from its conjunction with (B1).

How then *are* we to show that if all radical assurance is α- or β-assurance then α-assurance is impossible? Consider the conjunction of all those propositions which a man has α-assured himself to be true. Can we not somehow show that the man must also be α-assured that the conjunction itself is true and then deduce the impossibility of α-assurance from the impossibility of satisfying this requirement? For it is clearly not possible to satisfy this requirement, if all radical assurance is either α- or β-assurance. The man cannot be α-assured that the conjunction is true unless there is a proposition *h*, non-identical to the conjunction, which he has α-assured himself to be true and radically assured himself to be evidence for the conjunction. But he could not do the latter if *h* was an actual *conjunct* of the conjunction. You cannot radically assure yourself that *p* if *p* is false, and necessarily no proposition is evidence for a conjunction of which it is itself a member. And yet if *h* was a proposition of whose truth he was α-assured it would *have to be* a conjunct of the conjunction. For ex hypothesi the conjunction includes all the propositions of whose truth he is α-assured.

The trouble is that there seems no way to show that if you are α-assured of the truth of each of *p, q, r, . . .*, then you are also α-assured of the truth of the conjunction (*p*& *q*& *r*& . . .). You can be α-assured of the truth of each of *p, q, r, . . .* without even believing the conjunction (*p*& *q*& *r*& . . .); you may just not put the propositions together in a conjunctive object of belief. Should we say then that if you are α-assured that each of *p, q, r, . . .* is true, then it is at any rate logically possible that you are α-assured of the truth of the conjunction (*p*& *q*& *r*& . . .)? If we could say that much, then I think a modified version of the argument would probably succeed. But even that much seems arbitrary, on closer inspection. Why must it follow that it is logically possible for you to be α-*assured* of the truth of the conjunction, as distinct from just radically assured of its truth? And if radical assurance is sufficient, then the argument collapses. For you could be radically assured of the truth of the conjunction by being β-assured of its truth.

But although we cannot use this idea about conjunctions to show that if all radical assurance is either α- or β-assurance then α-assurance is impossible, we can I think use it to show that on the same general assumption about radical assurance, any proposition which you can α-assure yourself to be true is also one which you can β-assure yourself to be true. The principle we need in order to reach that conclusion is that if someone has the power to be radically assured that each of $p, q, r, \ldots$ is true, and if he has the power to entertain the conjunction $(p\& q\& r\& \ldots)$, then he has the power to be radically assured of the truth of the conjunction $(p\& q\& r\& \ldots)$ We use this principle to show that if all radical assurance is either α- or β-assurance, and if someone has the power to be α-assured that each of $p, q, r, \ldots$ is true, then if he has the power to entertain the conjunction $(p\& q\& r\& \ldots)$, he has the power to be β-assured of the truth of this conjunction and hence of the truth of each of its conjuncts. So if the conjunction contains every proposition he has the power to α-assure himself is true, then he will also have the power to β-assure himself of the truth of each of these propositions, provided he has the power to entertain their whole conjunction. But the proviso is absurd. Whether I have the power to β-assure myself that a proposition is true cannot depend on whether I am able to entertain a conjunction of which it is a conjunct. If I have the power to β-assure myself of the truth of each proposition in the conjunction I must have this power irrespective of any power I have to entertain or β-assure myself of the conjunction as a whole. So we can drop the proviso and say that any proposition which you can α-assure yourself to be true is also one which you can β-assure yourself to be true. I will now set out the argument in full, defining a man's α-conjunction as the non-repetitive conjunction of each of the propositions of whose truth he has the power to be α-assured.

(1) There is some proposition which N has the power to be α-assured is true

(2) N has an α-conjunction C (from (1))

(3) If you have the power to be radically assured that each of $p, q, r, \ldots$ is true, and if you have the power to entertain the conjunction $(p\& q\& r\& \ldots)$, then you have the power to be radically assured that $(p\& q\& r\& \ldots)$

(4) If N has the power to be α-assured that C, then there is a proposition h, non-identical to C, which he has the power to α-assure himself to be true, and the power to radically assure himself to be evidence for C

(5) Necessarily, if p is a conjunction and q is a conjunct of p then q is not evidence for p

(6) If N has the power to α-assure himself that h, then h is a conjunct of C

(from (2))

(7) N cannot radically assure himself that h is evidence for C

(from (5) and (6))

(8) N cannot α-assure himself that C

(from (4) and (7))

(9) If all radical assurance is either α- or β-assurance then if N has the power to be radically assured that C then he has the power to be β-assured that C

(from (8))

(10) If you have the power to β-assure yourself that a conjunction is true you have the power to β-assure yourself of the truth of each conjunct of that conjunction

(11) If all radical assurance is either α- or β-assurance and if N has the power to be radically assured that C then he has the power to β-assure himself of the truth of each proposition which he has the power to α-assure himself to be true

(from (9) and (10))

(12) If all radical assurance is either α- or β-assurance and if N has the power to entertain C, then he has the power to β-assure himself of the truth of each proposition which he has the power to α-assure himself to be true

(from (2), (3) and (11))

(13) The power to β-assure oneself that a proposition is true cannot be contingent on the power to entertain a conjunction of which it is a conjunct

(14) If all radical assurance is either α-assurance or β-assurance then N has the power to β-assure himself of the truth of each proposition which he has the power to α-assure himself is true

(from (12) and (13))

(5) follows from two things I said about evidence in the previous chapter, namely that no proposition is evidence for itself, and that if p is a conjunction and q is evidence for p then q is evidence for each conjunct of p (see pp. 27–8 above).

But it is one thing to say that (1)–(14) is a sound argument for the conclusion that if all radical assurance is either α- or β-assurance then any proposition which you can α-assure yourself to be true is also one which you can β-assure yourself to be true, another to say that it enables you to become β-assured of the truth of that conclusion about α- and β-assurance. β-assurance was what we were actually looking for, and it seems to be excluded, in the present case, by the assumptions which have to be made about the conditions under which powers of assurance are enjoyed. So perhaps it is better simply to take it as true, but not something we can be β-assured of, that α-assurance is ruled out by the temporal regress argument which I considered at the outset.

3

On wanting radical assurance

You will now I think be inclined to accept that there is little we can be radically assured of. If all radical assurance is either α-assurance or β-assurance then regressive difficulties eliminate α-assurance. And on plausible assumptions about the scope of self-evidence, there is little we can be β-assured of. The next thing I must try to show is that extensive radical assurance, or an extensive power to gain radical assurance, is nevertheless something we are liable to want. Positive arguments for this conclusion are developed in the present chapter, and it is defended against various misunderstandings in chapter 4. Chapter 5 is a final reconsideration of the scope of β-assurance.

The circumstances which reveal our liability to want radical assurance or the power to gain it, are circumstances of philosophical reflexion. In the investigations of everyday life or the empirical sciences, we are content enough with ordinary sensory assurance, not much concerned with the degree of regressiveness in our evidential assurance, certainly not worried that it is not ultra-regressive and relies at some point or other on unassured affirmation. But, as I argue in the first section of this chapter, philosophical reflexion about what you want of your belief-system as a whole reveals that many of the propositions you believe are ones for whose truth you are liable vainly to want radical assurance. And as I argue in the second section, reflexion on philosophical problems about the sources of knowledge reveals that you are liable to want the power to be radically assured of the truth of many of the kinds of propositions for which you have an ordinary non-radical sensory assurance of truth.

(1) Desiderata for a belief-system

You are liable vainly to want radical assurance of the truth of many of the propositions you believe. And this liability is revealed in philosophical reflexion about what you want of your belief-system as a whole. Before trying to make these theses at all precise, I will try first roughly to describe a train of thought which might at any rate easily emerge in reflexion of that kind.

Suppose then that, turning away from the investigation of particular propositions, actual or prospective parts of your belief-system, you begin to reflect more generally about what characteristics you would like your whole belief-system to have. You might recognise to begin with a division, in the propositions you believe, between those whose truth or falsity you find more or less a matter of indifference, and those which for one reason or another you do positively want to be true. It may not matter very much to you whether there is some falsity in the various random beliefs you have acquired about how glue works, or the problems which so-and-so's relations in the Midlands used to have with their central heating, but there will be a core, within your belief-system, of propositions whose truth-value you find practically or theoretically important. Let us call that subset of what you believe the essential core of your belief-system. Reflecting now that not everything in the essential core of your belief-system is likely to be true unless there are non-coincidental connexions between the circumstances of your believing and the truth of what you believe, you ask yourself whether you would prefer these connexions to obtain because you have yourself deliberately conducted investigations non-coincidentally connected with the truth of the beliefs they issue in or reinforce, or because of the causation of your belief by factors wholly outside your own control. I suspect that you would then prefer it to be conscious and deliberate investigation which is non-coincidentally connected with your believing the truth. I cannot think of any actual grounds for this preference, any more than I can think how one might support the equally likely preference for a world in which good is an intended consequence of free human action and not just an accident or upshot of changes we are constrained to undergo. But it does at any rate seem to me likely that you would, on considering the matter, have this preference.

So far, then, you have reached the position of recognising that you want to assure yourself of the truth of the essential core of your belief-system by investigations non-coincidentally connected with its truth. How far is this from recognising that you want radical assurance of the truth of the essential core of your belief-system?

You are radically assured that p if and only if (i) you have assured yourself that p; (ii) p is true; (iii) if your assurance that p is evidential then it is ultra-regressive; (iv) on gaining assurance that p you are conscious of the nature of the activity of investigation by means of which your assurance has been gained; (v) there is a non-coincidental relation between your activity of gaining assurance that p and the fact that in believing p you are believing what is true; and (vi) if your assurance that p is evidential then conditions (i)–(v) would still hold if we substituted for p any of those additional propositions whose truth you must be assured of in order for condition (iii) to be satisfied. It remains then for you to recognise that you want an assurance, for every member of the essential core of your belief-system, which satisfies conditions (iii), (iv) and (vi).

Why should you want your assurances to satisfy condition (iv)? Given the choice of achieving your goal with some understanding of how you achieve it, and achieving it blindly, you are I think likely, as another brute matter of fact, to prefer achievement with understanding.

Why should you want your assurances to satisfy condition (iii)? For them to satisfy condition (iii) is for them to be ultra-regressive whenever they are evidential. And evidential assurance that p is ultra-regressive if you are assured of the truth of all those other propositions which you affirm in gaining your evidential assurance that p. These other propositions must at least include a proposition which you affirm to be evidence for p, and the proposition that q is evidence for p. Whether this is all they comprise depends on whether or not your assurance that q and that q is evidence for p is also evidential (see pp. 32–3 above). That you are likely to want your assurances of truth to be ultra-regressive whenever they are evidential follows I think from the fact that you are likely, on thinking about it, not merely to want that the activities of investigation which give you these assurances should be non-coincidentally successful, but also to want *the assurance* that they are non-coincidentally successful. If an activity of gaining evidential assurance that p is to be non-coincidentally connected with the fact that in believing p you believe the truth, then all those other propositions which you thereby affirm, must actually be true. And if you recognise that this *is* a necessary condition for the absence of coincidence, and want there to be no coincidence, then you will want to assure yourself that the necessary condition is satisfied. But to assure yourself that the necessary condition is satisfied is to assure yourself of the truth of all the propositions which you affirm in gaining your evidential assurance that *p*. And to succeed in *that* operation is to make your evidential assurance that *p* ultra-regressive.

Finally, the condition (vi) that if your assurance that *p* is evidential then conditions (i)–(v) would still hold if we substituted for *p* any of those additional propositions whose truth you must be assured of in order for *p* to satisfy condition (iii). If *p* belongs to the essential core of your belief-system then you want it to satisfy (ii). And I have suggested that you will also want *p* to satisfy (i) and (iii)–(v) when it belongs to the essential core of your belief-system. But if *q* is any of those additional propositions whose truth you must be assured of in order for *p* to satisfy (iii), and you want *p* to satisfy (iii), then, presumably *q* thereby also belongs to the essential core of your belief-system, is a proposition believed by you and whose truth-value you do not find a matter of indifference. So you want *q* to satisfy (i)–(v), and hence *p* to satisfy (vi).

Given the general verisimilitude of the train of thought or process of introspection which I have just been describing, we can now move on to a more formal argument for your liability to want radical assurance of the truth of the essential core of your belief-system.

It will simplify matters if I introduce a bit more technical jargon. By '*N* is directly liable to believe *p* (not to believe *p*)' I shall mean '*N* would be likely to believe *p* (not to believe *p*) if he entertained it'. By '*N* is indirectly liable to believe *p* (not to believe *p*)' I shall mean '*N* would be likely to believe *p* (not to believe *p*) if he made an impartial investigation into its truth-value'. By '*N* is *A*-liable to want *x* (not to want *x*)' I shall mean '*N* would be likely to want *x* (not to want *x*) if he entertained the possibility of getting it'. By '*N* is *B*-liable to want *x* (not to want *x*)' I shall mean 'There is something which *N* is *A*-liable to want, and either there is at least one proposition which *N* is indirectly liable to believe and such that if *N* wanted what he is *A*-liable to want and believed the proposition(s), then he would be likely to want *x* (not to want *x*), or there is at least one proposition which *N* is indirectly liable not to believe and such that if *N* wanted what he is *A*-liable to want and did not believe the proposition(s), then he would be likely to want *x* (not to want *x*)'. Putting things in these terms, it is I think possible to show that you are *B*-liable to want radical assurance of the truth of every member of the essential core of your belief-system. The argument is as follows:

(1) You are *A*-liable to want to assure yourself of the truth of the essential core of your belief-system by means of investigations non-coincidentally connected with its truth

(2) You are *A*-liable to want the assurance you gain to be accompanied by consciousness of the nature of the activity by which you have gained it

(3) You are *A*-liable to want assurance that you have gained assurance, by means of investigations non-coincidentally connected with its truth, of the truth of the essential core of your belief-system

(4) You are indirectly liable to believe that the wants referred to in (1)–(3) cannot be satisfied unless you have radical assurance of the truth of the essential core of your belief-system

(5) You are *B*-liable to want radical assurance of the truth of the essential core of your belief-system (from (1)–(4))

The argument is valid, given my definitions of *A*- and *B*-liability. The wants which (1)–(3) say you are *A*-liable to have are ones which you would be likely to have, consciously, when entertaining propositions about what you want of your belief-system as a whole. (4) I would defend by the considerations I mentioned when describing the original train of thought.

Each *A*-liability statement in (1)–(3) corresponds to a conditional. And the antecedents of these conditionals will be true only if you engage in a certain kind of philosophical reflexion. But entering on the reflexion itself is too easy and natural for the consequents of the conditionals to be a matter of indifference. One hardly needs a special justification for asking what one wants of one's belief-system as a whole, in the way that one needs a justification for undertaking the Cartesian project of ascertaining which parts of one's belief-system are immediately or derivatively certain.[1] And if you are indeed *B*-liable to want radical assurance of the truth of the essential core of your belief-system, you are clearly *B*-liable to want much more radical assurance than my previous conclusions about its availability allow you to get. Taken in conjunction with these conclusions, (1)–(5) supports a non-arbitrary scepticism.

It is natural at this point to wonder whether the desire for radical

[1] Cf. Williams (1978) Ch. 2

assurance of the truth of the essential core of your belief-system could really be anything but an idle wish, like wanting to have written *Hamlet*, or wanting to have a perfect knowledge of every European language. But what is it that makes for serious wanting, as opposed to mere idle wishing? Is it that if you believe that at least one means to the satisfaction of your want is in fact available, there is at least one means which you are really willing to make use of and whose attendant costs you are really willing to pay? That does indeed seem to be a necessary condition for wanting something seriously, but it is not a condition we should expect to be violated when what you want is something which you believe it impossible for you to have. If I now want to have written *Hamlet*, there are no means to the satisfaction of my desire which I am likely to think presently available. And similarly if I want radical assurance of the truth of the essential core of my belief-system. Nor is the mere belief that it is not now possible for some state of affairs to obtain sufficient in itself to prevent you from seriously wanting it to obtain. I can certainly now want, as seriously as you like, that some past event should never have happened.

Is it possible for N to be willing, at t, to do x if certain circumstances were to occur, and at the same time to believe that it is impossible for these circumstances to occur? If so, then we could make it a condition for seriously wanting something that, whether or not you believe it is possible for you to have it, you are now willing to give up something you now enjoy in exchange for having it. But even if this is an intelligible condition for serious wanting, I do not think it will prevent you from seriously wanting more radical assurance than you believe it is possible for you to have. On separately considering each of the severally necessary and jointly sufficient conditions for you to have radical assurance of the truth of the essential core of your belief-system, you would I think be willing to give up something in order for that condition to be satisfied. Why should you change your mind on recognising that, because of the actual content of the essential core of your belief-system, the conditions are not all jointly satisfiable?

Willingness to pay actual or hypothetical costs of getting what you want may well not be a sufficient condition for wanting it seriously. Suppose you are willing to give up something you now enjoy in order to have a perfect knowledge of every European language. You might be equally willing to give up only negligibly less for a perfect knowledge of every European language other than, say, Romanian and Flemish, or possibly even for a good knowledge of French, German, Spanish, Italian, Russian, Polish and Hungarian. This makes your desire for a perfect knowledge of every European language the gratuitous exaggeration of a more modest want. In the same way, the 'Cartesian' desire to believe only those propositions whose falsity is logically impossible or inconsistent with the fact that you believe them might be a gratuitous exaggeration of the more modest desire to believe only what is true, or the even more modest desire that the essential core of your belief-system should be true. Is the desire for radical assurance of the essential core of your belief-system similarly unserious, reducible quite painlessly to a more modest desire, or even to a desire which we might actually be able to satisfy? Wanting radical assurance of the truth of everything you believe might well be a gratuitous exaggeration of wanting radical assurance of the essential core of your belief-system. But I cannot identify any more modest and satisfiable desire which this latter desire gratuitously exaggerates.

To say that philosophical reflexion reveals a liability to want more radical assurance than you are able to have is not of course to say that radical assurance is something you 'need', or something which it is *good* to have or want. Nor is it to claim that you are able to provide an actual rationale for wanting radical assurance, or that there is no true proposition, or even proposition of whose truth you can be radically assured, the believing of which would diminish the desire for radical assurance which philosophical reflexion may lead you into. Even if scepticism about radical assurance is both true and non-arbitrary, there may still be consolations for believing it. I will take up questions about needing radical assurance in the first section of the next chapter, and questions of consolation in Chapter 8.

(2) *Sources of knowledge*

Traditionally, there are four sources of knowledge. As Reid puts it 'the faculties of consciousness, of memory, of external sense, and of reason are all equally the gifts of nature. No good reason can be assigned for receiving the testimony of one of them, which is not of equal force with regard to the others.'[1] But the question arises of

[1] Thomas Reid *Essays on the Intellectual Powers* p. 439 (quoted in Chisholm (1977) p. 122)

whether there are not other faculties as well, which enable us to gain moral, aesthetic, or religious knowledge, and this through an experience which resembles ordinary sensory experience in that propositions to the effect that such experience occurs are evidence for the independent existence of states of affairs which bear at least some resemblance to the intentional object of the experience itself.[1] Now the question would be settled if we had the power to be radically assured that there is non-sensory moral or religious or aesthetic experience, and that propositions affirming the occurrence of such experience have an evidential role analogous to that of propositions to the effect that ordinary sensory experience occurs. On my initial assumptions about the scope of self-evidence we do not have the necessary power of gaining radical assurance. But I think that unless you had an entirely unlooked-for degree of confidence in these assumptions you would still want the powers of radical assurance necessary for settling the question about the sources of knowledge, provided only that you were not certain that you already had the power necessary to settle that question in some other way. And if, lacking this certainty, you did want these powers to be radically assured of the truth of the relevant propositions about moral or religious or aesthetic experience, then I think you would also be liable to want the power to gain radical assurance of the truth of the analogous propositions about ordinary sensory experience, and hence the power to gain radical assurance of the truth of many of the kinds of propositions for which we have sensory assurance, and hence many of the propositions which we actually believe. For it would be hard to believe that these latter powers would not be concomitants of your expanded powers of radical assurance with respect to propositions about moral or religious or aesthetic experience. And you *are* liable to be uncertain that you have the power to settle the original question about these kinds of experience in some way other than the hypothetical method of using extra powers of radical assurance. And so the sceptic, in his effort to show that our incapacity to gain much radical assurance is a more than trivial lack, need not rely solely on our liability to want actual radical assurance when reflecting about the desiderata of our belief-system as a whole. We are liable to want a power radically to assure ourselves of the truth of propositions for which we have sensory assurance. And we are liable to want this power not for its own sake, or because sensory

[1] For explanations of this terminology see pp. 19–20 above

assurance leaves a residue of doubt which can only be banished by assurance of a more self-conscious kind, but because we find it difficult to believe that its possession would not be the concomitant of possessing a power to resolve quite genuine doubts about non-sensory experiences and sources of knowledge.

This at any rate is the thought I shall try now to develop, taking as an example the claim to religious knowledge through non-sensory mystical experience. But the thought is not at all easy to unfold into a properly surveyable argument, and premisses will in any case emerge which it would take a complete theological treatise to defend. Readers sufficiently convinced by the previous section may therefore prefer to move straight on to Chapter 4, in which the thesis of our liability to want actual radical assurance is related to various current doctrines about infinite justificatory regression.

(a) *Evidence and experience*

I will say that a proposition is OS-existential if it is to the effect that there occurs, has occurred, or will occur a particular sensory experience whose intentional object is outer and concrete. 'It looks to me as if there is a man in the doorway' could express an OS-existential proposition: it entails that a visual experience occurs and the content of this experience cannot be fully specified except by a description which, if it referred to something existing independently of the experience, would refer to something outside my mind and spatio-temporally located (see pp. 19–20 above). I will say also that a proposition is OS-evidential if it is of the form 'q is evidence for p', where q is OS-existential and p to the effect that there is an independently existing state of affairs which bears at least some resemblance to the intentional object of the experience referred to by q. OS-existential and OS-evidential propositions must now be compared with those even more artificial propositions which result if we substitute for 'sensory experience whose intentional object is outer and concrete' 'mystical experience whose intentional object is an independently existing God'. They must be compared, in a heartless extension of the abbreviatory jargon, with M-existential and M-evidential propositions. These M-propositions are more artificial than the corresponding OS-propositions because although one might, outside philosophy, claim that things look to one to be a certain way without saying so much as that one sees that that is how they are, or so little as that one believes that that is how they are, the mystic is more likely either to claim an actually veridical non-sensory experience of an independently existing God, an 'infused and loving knowledge', or merely wonder whether the whole episode was not a more or less sinister illusion. But, once we have actually introduced the notion of M-existential and M-evidential propositions, corresponding to OS-existential and OS-evidential propositions, we will want to assure ourselves about whether any such propositions are true. More particularly, we will want to assure ourselves about the truth-value of

(1) There are true M-evidential propositions, referring to true M-existential propositions and to the effect that the M-existential propositions they refer to are evidence for the independent existence of something very like the intentional object of the experiences referred to by the M-existential propositions themselves

For the mystic's actual claim to veridical non-sensory experience of an independently existing God cannot be true unless (1) is true, any more than it can be true that I see a man in the doorway unless the OS-existential proposition 'it looks to me as if there is a man in the doorway' is both true and evidence for 'there is a man in the doorway' (see pp. 19–20 above).

There are various ways in which it might occur to you that you can adequately assure yourself of the truth-value of (1). Perhaps you can reveal an incoherence in the notion of non-sensory experience, or in any notion of God which could be used to indicate the intentional object of the experience an M-existential proposition referred to. Perhaps you can adduce the Kierkegaardian doctrine that nothing is worthy of the name of God of whose existence we could be evidentially assured. Perhaps the existence of true M-evidential propositions is ruled out by scepticism about the evidential role of experiential propositions of any kind; maybe no proposition to the effect that a particular experience occurs can be evidence for the independent existence of anything like the intentional object of the experience unless there is independent evidence for its independent existence; or maybe all experience is too 'theory-laden' for any proposition to the effect that a particular experience occurs to be evidence for the independent existence of anything like its intentional object.

Alternatively, you might think you can assure yourself that (1) is true by appealing to the analogy between OS-propositions and M-propositions, and to our ability to gain a satisfactory kind of assurance of the truth of OS-propositions. Spurning the considerations I set out in the first section of this chapter, about wants liable to emerge in reflexion about ideal total belief-systems, you might claim there is no reason to doubt that inner sense gives you a perfectly satisfactory non-radical assurance of the truth of OS-existential propositions, and that you also have some satisfactory way of assuring yourself that OS-evidential propositions are true. Inner sense gives you a satisfactory though non-radical assurance that this OS-existential proposition about your visual experience is evidence for the independent existence of a man in the doorway. But now, if you do have these powers with respect to OS-propositions, and if the theological and general epistemological considerations already referred to do not enable you to establish the falsity of M-existential or M-evidential propositions, then surely you also have powers to assure yourself that the M-propositions are true. For if the mystic claims an inner sense by means of which he can assure himself that M-existential propositions are true, in something of the way that you can assure yourself through inner sense that OS-existential propositions are true, why should his claim not give you a perfectly satisfactory evidential assurance of the truth of M-existential propositions? And why should it not be possible for you to assure yourself that M-evidential propositions are true in the same way that you assure yourself that OS-evidential propositions are true?

Or again, you might imagine, contrary to my initial assumption about the scope of self-evidence, that both M-existential and M-evidential propositions are ones which people can β-assure themselves to be true. Thus, either you can β-assure yourself that (1) is true, or you can β-assure yourself that M-evidential propositions are true, and gain non-radical evidential assurance that M-existential propositions are true by accepting the reports of a mystic who was able to 'see' the truth of M-existential propositions referring to his own experiences. I will refer to these possibilities collectively as the method of β-assurance.

Now suppose that although you are not sure that any of the methods I have so far mentioned, or any other method you can think of, actually will give you a satisfactory assurance of (1)'s truth-value, you can think of one or more methods of whose inefficacy in this respect you are also not sure. Then I think that each method, of whose inefficacy you are thus uncertain, will be one which you want to be effective, want to be capable of giving you a satisfactory assurance of (1)'s truth-value. But it seems to me that you are indeed unlikely, on reflexion, to be sure that any of the methods I mentioned, or any other method, will give you a satisfactory assurance of (1)'s truth-value, and at the same time unlikely to be sure that all of the methods I mentioned are ineffective, and in particular unlikely to be sure that the method of β-assurance is ineffective. My initial assumptions about the scope of self-evidence were I hope plausible. But still the scope of self-evidence is not a matter on which any reflective person is likely to reach certainty. Now, if you want something then you are liable also to want what you are liable to believe is an inevitable concomitant of the satisfaction of that want. But you are liable to believe that if M-existential propositions really were such that you or the man having the experience they specify has the power to be β-assured of their truth, then you would also have the power to be β-assured of the truth of OS-existential propositions referring to your own experiences. You will for example be inclined to think that if the man having a mystical experience, whose intentional object is a transcendent God, can, after all and despite my initial assumptions about self-evidence, 'see' that he is having this experience, then surely the man having an ordinary sensory experience will likewise be able simply to 'see' that he is having this sensory experience. And similarly, you are liable to believe that if you really did have the power to be β-assured of the truth of M-evidential propositions, then you would also have the power to be β-assured of the truth of OS-evidential propositions. So you are liable to want the power to be radically assured of the truth of OS-evidential propositions referring to OS-existential propositions referring to your own experiences.

If I am right so far, then there is a relatively easy and mechanical route from here to the conclusion that you are liable to want the power to be radically assured of the truth of many of the kinds of propositions of whose truth you have sensory assurance, and from there to the further conclusion that often, when you believe a proposition, you are liable to want the power to be radically assured of the truth of propositions of that kind. And it is also easy enough to restate the whole argument in the more precise terminology of A-

and B-liability which I introduced in the previous section. But these further developments can be postponed until the second part of this section. The prior task is to defend the actual heart of the argument.

Two main kinds of objections need to be considered. There is the objection that we can after all quite clearly reach adequate assurance of (1)'s truth-value by some method other than the method of β-assurance. And there are objections to the psychology I tacitly appealed to in moving to my final conclusion about OS-propositions from your supposed agnosticism about methods of gaining assurance of (1)'s truth-value. I will begin with the psychology.

I assumed that if you do not believe that you can gain assurance of (1)'s truth-value by any method, but if there are one or more methods of whose inefficacy you are not quite sure, then you will want to gain the assurance by each method about whose inefficacy you have this uncertainty. This assumption is not incompatible with my previous claim that you can quite seriously want something which you believe that you cannot get (see p. 71 above). You could still want assurance of (1)'s truth-value even if you were quite sure that you could never have it and hence that there was no effective method of gaining it. But if you are to want something purely as a means to an end, then you cannot be sure that it is an ineffective means. For otherwise there would be no limit to what you wanted as a means to the achievement of things you wanted but did not believe you could actually achieve. It follows also that if one is to want something purely as a means to an end one cannot be sure that the end is unattainable (cf. p. 71 above). This is why I must argue from the hypothesis that you are not sure that you can gain assurance of (1)'s truth-value, as distinct from the hypothesis that you are sure that you cannot gain assurance of its truth-value.

I also assumed that if one wants something one is liable to want what one believes is an inevitable concomitant of the satisfaction of that want. If you find this principle implausible, then you are probably taking it to imply that one looks forward to what one believes to be the inevitable concomitants of gaining what one wants with a satisfaction independent of the satisfaction with which one looks forward to gaining what one believes they are concomitants of. But the principle does not imply this, and is in fact compatible with the supposition that one would have viewed the concomitants with unmitigated hostility if one had not believed them to be concomitants, or had not wanted what one believes them to be concomitants of, and even that just because one would have had this attitude towards them, one does not want to want what one believes them to be concomitants of.

I come back now to the objection that we can after all quite clearly reach adequate assurance, by some method other than the method of β-assurance, of the truth-value of

(1) There are true M-evidential propositions, referring to true M-existential propositions and to the effect that the true M-existential propositions they refer to are evidence for the independent existence of something very like the intentional object of the experiences referred to by the M-existential propositions themselves

It is obviously impossible, within my present scope, adequately to criticise even one of the various conceivable methods of reaching assurance of (1)'s truth-value which I mentioned earlier. But it may at least be appropriate to make a few remarks on the attempt to reach assurance of (1)'s falsity by appealing to doubts about the evidential role of experiential propositions in general.

Doubts of that kind might be based on the principle that no proposition entailing the occurrence of any kind of experience, sensory or non-sensory, can be evidence for the independent existence of anything like the intentional object of this experience unless there is independent evidence for its independent existence. Something close to this principle can be seen at work in for example Ayer's comment on 'the version of the causal theory of perception which turns physical objects into unobservable occupants of an unobservable space'. 'The decisive objection', he writes,

> is that if this were so we should have no means of identifying (the physical objects), and if we had no means of identifying them, we should have no reason to believe that they played any part in the production of our sensations, or even that they existed at all. The point which advocates of this position have overlooked is that physical objects cannot be identified in the first instance as the causes of our sensations: they have to be independently identified before we can have any right to say that the causal relation holds.[1]

[1] Ayer (1973) p. 87

As Mackie remarks, our confidence in this kind of argument

> may be somewhat shaken by the consideration that modern
> physics seems systematically to violate its principles. Various
> aspects of the behaviour of large-scale things are explained as
> being caused by the doings of atomic and sub-atomic particles,
> but the latter are never directly observed, being rather inferred
> from the observation of those large-scale performances which
> they are supposed to cause and hence to explain. Are not the
> physicists guilty of using causal inferences in terms of laws, which
> cannot have been independently established by the direct observa-
> tion of the causes in question being followed by their supposed
> effects ?[1]

But for present purposes it would perhaps in any case suffice to
emphasise the distinction between the thesis that q is evidence for p
and the thesis that we can assure ourselves that q is evidence for p.
Maybe we cannot assure ourselves that any proposition to the effect
that experience occurs is evidence for the independent existence of
something like the intentional object of that experience. But it cannot
possibly follow that no experiential propositions have this evidential role.

Finally, there is the objection that experience, sensory or otherwise, is too much dependent on conceptual schemes or belief-
systems, too 'theory-laden', for any proposition entailing the
occurrence of a particular experience to be evidence for the independent existence of anything like the intentional object of the
experience. The thought is vague enough. One possible interpretation is this. I have to apply a concept in order to have an experience
at all; I can for instance have a retinal reaction without applying a
concept, but not a visual experience. A tree can affect my retina even
if I have no concept of a tree, but unless I possess and make use of
this concept I cannot see that there is a tree before me and neither
can it look to me as if there is. But if, by deliberately altering my
conceptual scheme, I can alter experiences I have, how can a proposition to the effect that I enjoy such and such an experience be evidence for a proposition entailing the existence of an object independent of my will ?

The objection is confused. Suppose we define 'x is independent of
my will' to mean 'it is not within my power to make it either true or

[1] Mackie (1976) pp. 62–3

false that x exists, or more or less likely that x exists'. And suppose we let q stand for a proposition which is (i) non-deductive evidence for 'x exists', where x is independent of my will, and (ii) a proposition to the effect that I have a certain experience. Certainly it is not within my power to make a proposition like q *true* by altering my conceptual scheme, because if it is then it is also within my power to make it more likely that 'x exists' is true, which conflicts with the assumption that x is independent of my will. This is because, on the usage I explained in Chapter 1, 'there is a proposition which is non-deductive evidence for p' entails 'there is a proposition such that when a proposition like it is true so usually at least is a proposition like p' (see p. 28 above). There is on the other hand no conflict between the assumption that x is independent of my will and the proposition that it is within my power, by altering my conceptual scheme, to make propositions like q *false*. For it does not follow, from my having that power, that I have the power to make it less likely that x exists. 'There is a false proposition which is non-deductive evidence for p' does not entail 'there is a proposition such that when a proposition like it is false, so usually at least is a proposition like p'. But now, there is surely no reason to think that my power to alter the experiences I have by deliberately altering my conceptual scheme is a power to make myself have certain experiences I would not otherwise have had; it is at most a power to prevent myself from having experiences I would otherwise have had. 'Power to alter the experiences I have' must accordingly be interpreted so that the enjoyment of this power is consistent with there being true *OS*-existential propositions which are evidence for the existence of objects independent of my will.

There seems to be only one other plausible interpretation of the theory-ladenness objection, namely that I cannot actually enjoy the experience described by the proposition which I cite as evidence for a proposition entailing the existence of an object independent of my will unless, paradoxically, this latter proposition is one which I already believe. For example, it cannot even look to me as if there is a tree in front of me unless I already believe, albeit hesitantly, that there is indeed a tree in front of me. Why should this make it inappropriate for me to cite the experiential proposition as evidence for the proposition about the independent object? If q is evidence for p then it is not the case that any normally intelligent man who was doubtful about p would thereby be made equally doubtful about q. But if it cannot look to me as if there is a tree in front of me unless I believe that there is, and if we also assume that I cannot believe that it looks to me as if there is unless it looks to me as if there is, it will be just as difficult for me to believe that it looks to me as if there is as for me to believe that there is. Hence the proposition that it looks to me as if there is a tree in front of me cannot be evidence for the proposition that there is a tree in front of me. But of course we need some reason for accepting that its looking to me as if there is a tree in front of me requires me to believe, even hesitantly, that there is indeed such a tree. Might it not just be that sentences of the form 'there looks to be a ϕ' are normally used for the two quite separate purposes of asserting one's inclination to believe that there is a ϕ, and describing one's visual experiences?

(b) *Re-statement of the argument*

The first part of this section may have convinced you that a sound and full argument could in time be constructed for the thesis that we are liable to want the power to be radically assured of the truth of both OS-evidential propositions and the OS-existential propositions they refer to.[1] But the nature of that argument has been only very sketchily indicated, the thesis itself is vague, and I also originally intended to reach the rather stronger conclusion that often, when you believe a proposition, you are liable to want the power to be radically assured of the truth of propositions of that kind. I will now try to recapitulate the first part of the section with a little more exactitude, and move also to the stronger conclusion which I originally intended to reach. What follows can be treated very much as an appendix, and can certainly be omitted by anyone either entirely convinced or entirely unconvinced by the first part of the section.

In section (1) of this chapter I defined direct and indirect liability to believe something, and A- and B-liability to want something. N is directly liable to believe p (not to believe p) if and only if he would be likely to believe p (not to believe p) if he entertained it. N is

---

[1] OS-existential propositions were to the effect that there occurs, has occurred or will occur a particular sensory experience whose intentional object is outer and concrete; OS-evidential propositions were of the form 'q is evidence for p', where q is OS-existential and p to the effect that there is an independently existing state of affairs which bears at least some resemblance to the intentional object of the experience referred to by q.

indirectly liable to believe p (not to believe p) if and only if he would be likely to believe p (not to believe p) if he made an impartial investigation into its truth-value. N is A-liable to want x (not to want x) if and only if N would be likely to want x (not to want x) if he entertained the possibility of getting it. N is B-liable to want x (not to want x) if and only if there is something which N is A-liable to want and either there is at least one proposition which N is indirectly liable to believe and such that if N wanted what he is A-liable to want and believed the proposition(s), then he would be likely to want x (not to want x), or there is at least one proposition which N is indirectly liable not to believe and such that if N wanted what he is A-liable to want and did not believe the proposition(s), then he would be likely to want x (not to want x). In these terms my present suggestions are that

(A) You are B-liable to want the power to be radically assured of the truth of both OS-evidential propositions and the OS-existential propositions which they refer to

that if (A) is true then so is

(B) You are B-liable to want the power to be radically assured of the truth of many of the kinds of propositions of whose truth you have sensory assurance

and that if (B) is true then so is

(C) Often, when you believe a proposition, you are B-liable to want the power to be radically assured of the truth of propositions of that kind

The 'if (B) then (C)' hypothetical is I think clear without argument. You need only accept that we do often have sensory assurance of truth.

For the 'if (A) then (B) hypothetical' I start by isolating the proposition

(P1) The power to gain radical assurance of the truth of much for which you have sensory assurance is an inevitable concomitant of the power to gain radical assurance of the truth of OS-evidential propositions and the OS-existential propositions they refer to

We then have:

(1) If you are *B*-liable to want *a* and if '*b* is an inevitable concomitant of *a*' stands for a true proposition which you are indirectly liable to believe, then you are β-liable to want *b*

(2) If (A), and if (P1) is a true proposition which you are indirectly liable to believe, then (B)

(from (1))

(3) (P1) is a true proposition which you are indirectly liable to believe

(4) If (A) then (B)

(from (2) and (3))

Why (1)? If you are *B*-liable to want *x* then there is an object which you are *A*-liable to want and one or more propositions which you are indirectly liable to believe, such that if you wanted the object and believed the set of propositions you would be likely to want *x*. Suppose that you would want *b* if you wanted *a* and believed that *b* was an inevitable concomitant of *a*. Then if you were likely to want *a* you would be likely to want *b*. Suppose further that '*b* is an inevitable concomitant of *a*' stands for a proposition which you are indirectly liable to believe. If, under these suppositions, you were *B*-liable to want *a*, there would be an object which you were *A*-liable to want, and the propositions which you were indirectly liable to believe would include '*b* is an inevitable concomitant of *a*'. Furthermore, the object which you were *A*-liable to want and the propositions which you were indirectly liable to believe would be such that if you wanted the object and believed the propositions, you would be likely to want *b* as well as *a*. Hence, by the definition of *B*-liability, you would be *B*-liable to want *b* as well as *B*-liable to want *a*. So (1) will be true if it is true in general that if you want one thing and believe that a second thing is an inevitable concomitant of getting the first, then you also want the second thing. I defended this principle in the first part of the section (see pp. 78–9 above).

(3) says that it is true, and a proposition you are indirectly liable to believe, that

(P1) The power to gain radical assurance of the truth of much for which you have sensory assurance is an inevitable concomitant of the power to gain radical assurance of the truth of *OS*-evidential propositions and the *OS*-existential propositions they refer to

Is (P1) true? It follows from the assumptions about sense-perception which I introduced in Chapter 1 that you cannot have outer sensory assurance that p unless there is a true OS-existential proposition q and a true OS-evidential proposition to the effect that q is evidence for a proposition whose existential implications bear at least some resemblance to those of p (see pp. 20–21 above). I allowed that the resemblance might be no more than partial because I did not want to commit myself on the theory of primary and secondary qualities. But even on the most generous view of what falls on the secondary side of the division, there will be many cases in which the proposition which q is evidence for is in fact identical to p. If this is right, then (P1) will be true unless it is possible to have the power to be radically assured that q and that q is evidence for p, and yet lack the power to be radically assured that p. It seems to me that you would only have the one power and lack the other if you somehow lacked the power to think of the three propositions 'q', 'q is evidence for p' and 'p' all together, and this seems impossible given that 'q is evidence for p' itself refers to the other two propositions and must itself be thought of if you are to be radically assured of its truth. And having said all this, I must of course also say that (P1) is a proposition which you are indirectly liable to believe, one which you would be likely to believe if you made an impartial investigation into its truth-value.

It does seem then that

(B) You are B-liable to want the power to be radically assured of the truth of many of the kinds of propositions of whose truth you have sensory assurance

if it is also true that

(A) You are B-liable to want the power to be radically assured of the truth of both OS-evidential propositions and the OS-existential propositions they refer to

(A) is the conclusion which I was in effect arguing for in the first part of this section. And I now offer a more formal and explicit version of that argument. We can begin by isolating the proposition

(P2) There are true M-evidential propositions, referring to true M-existential propositions and to the effect that the true M-existential propositions they refer to are evidence for the independent existence of something very like the intentional object of the experiences referred to by the M-existential propositions themselves

We now have the following argument:

(a) You are A-liable to want assurance about the truth-value of mystics' claims to have non-sensory experiences of union with an independently existing God

If (a) is true then so is

(b) You are B-liable to want the power to assure yourself about the truth-value of (P2)

And if (b) is true then so is

(A) You are B-liable to want the power to be radically assured of the truth of both OS-evidential propositions and the OS-existential propositions they refer to

(a) I take as axiomatic, but arguments are necessary for 'if (a) then (b)' and 'if (B) then (A)'.

Why should we accept that if (a) is true so is (b)? Consider the proposition

(P3) You can assure yourself about the truth-value of the mystics' claims if and only if you have the power to assure yourself about the truth-value of (P2)

If you believed (P3) and wanted to assure yourself about the truth-value of the mystics' claims then you would be likely to want to assure yourself about the truth-value of (P2). But (P3) is a proposition which you are indirectly liable to believe. And (a) says that you are directly liable to want to assure yourself about the truth-value of the mystics' claims. So if (a) is true, so is

(b) You are B-liable to want to assure yourself about the truth-value of (P2)

Why, finally, should we accept that if (b) is true so is

(A) You are B-liable to want to gain the power to be radically assured of the truth of both OS-evidential propositions and the OS-existential propositions they refer to?

I begin by isolating the propositions

(P4) It is certain that there is a method by which you can satisfactorily assure yourself of the truth-value of (P2)

(P5) It is certain that you cannot satisfactorily assure yourself of (P2)'s truth-value in the way that you would be able to if someone could be β-assured of the truth of M-existential propositions and you could be β-assured of the truth of M-evidential propositions

and

(P6) If you had the power to assure yourself of the truth-value of (P2) by the method mentioned in (P5) then you would inevitably also have the power to be radically assured of the truth of both OS-evidential propositions and the OS-existential propositions they refer to

We now have the following argument:

(1) If you are B-liable to want to do a then you are B-liable to want to do a by method X if the following formulae stand for propositions which you are indirectly liable not to believe: it is certain that a can be done by some method; it is certain that a cannot be done by method X

(2) If you are B-liable to want to do a by method X, then you are B-liable to want the power to do b if the following formula stands for a proposition which you are indirectly liable to believe: the power to do b is an inevitable concomitant of the power to do a by method X

(3) If (b) and you are indirectly liable not to believe (P4) and indirectly liable not to believe (P5) then you are B-liable to want the power to assure yourself of (P2)'s truth-value by the method of β-assurance mentioned in (P5)

(from (1))

(4) If you are B-liable to want the power to assure yourself of (P2)'s truth-value by the method of β-assurance mentioned in (P5) then (A)

(from (2))

(5) You are indirectly liable not to believe (P4) and indirectly liable not to believe (P5) and indirectly liable to believe (P6)

(6) If (b) then (A)

(from (3) (4) and (5))

The argument for (1) is partly parallel to my earlier argument for
the proposition that if you are B-liable to want a and if 'B is an
inevitable concomitant of a' stands for a true proposition which you
are indirectly liable to believe then you are B-liable to want b (see
p. 86 above). Suppose that if you were likely to want to do a and
did not believe either that there was certainly a method by which
you could do a or that it was certain that a could not be done by
method X, then you would be likely to want to do a by method X.
Suppose further that 'it is certain that you can do a by some method'
and 'it is certain that you cannot do a by method X' stand for
propositions which you are indirectly liable not to believe. If under
these suppositions you were B-liable to want the power to do a,
there would be some object which you were A-liable to want, and
the propositions which you were indirectly liable not to believe
would include 'it is certain that you can do a by some method' and
'it is certain that you cannot do a by method X'. Furthermore, the
object which you were A-liable to want and the propositions you
were indirectly liable not to believe would be such that if you wanted
to do a and did not believe these propositions then you would be
likely not merely to want to do a but also to want to do a by method
X. Hence by the definition of B-liability you will be B-liable to
want to do a by method X. So (1) will be true if we grant the
psychological assumption that if you want to do a and are not sure
that there is some method by which you can do a and are not sure
that you cannot do a by method X then you will want to do a by
method X. And by a similar argument (2) will be true if we grant the
psychological assumption that if you want to do a by method X and
believe that the power to do b is an inevitable concomitant of having
the power to do a by method X then you want the power to do b. I
have nothing to add to what I said in favour of these two psychological assumptions in the first part of the section (see pp. 78–9 above),
and nothing to add either to what I said there against (P4) (see pp.
79–82 above) and (P5) (see p. 77 above) and in favour of (P6) (see
p. 77 above).

4

Infinite justificatory regression: some pseudo-solutions

Radical assurance is a species of what we ordinarily call justified belief (see p. 42 above). And the sceptical doctrine about radical assurance which we have now finally reached is one interpretation – I think the only plausible and disturbing interpretation – of the vaguer and more general doctrine that for much of what we believe an infinite regress of justification is both necessary and impossible. Chapter 2 gave us a version of the impossibility half of the doctrine: the regressive demands of radical and evidential assurance were on plausible assumptions about the scope of self-evidence hardly ever possible to satisfy. Chapter 3 gave us two separate versions of the necessity half: you are liable to want radical assurance of the truth of every member of the essential core of your belief-system, and you are independently liable to want the power to be radically assured of the truth of many of the kinds of propositions for which you have sensory assurance of truth. But one of the main concerns of current epistemology is precisely to explain how regresses of justification can after all be sufficiently often terminated or avoided. So for example there is the common suggestion that justificatory regresses can be terminated by the believing of propositions for which justification is simply not 'needed'. Another popular suggestion is that they can be terminated by the actual having of experience. There are also the vaguer beliefs current that regressive difficulties stem somehow from failure to appreciate the role of *coherence* in justified believing, from the acceptance of some long-exploded 'foundational' or 'linear' theory of justification, or from failure to appreciate the extent to which justified believing is a matter not so much of providing positive evidence as of meeting criticisms and objections. My argument will be more plausible if I can persuade you of the falsity or irrelevance of these various current doctrines. Section (1) of this chapter is on the no-need theory, section (2) is on justification by experience, section (3) is on foundationalism and coherence and section (4) is on Critical Rationalism.

(1) *Needing and wanting assurance*

There is a division, among writers who offer a stopping-place for regresses of justification, between those who say that you cannot be inferentially justified in believing *p* unless you are also justified in believing the proposition which you take as evidence for *p*, and those who say that sometimes, and even for the believing of what you cite as evidence, justification is simply not 'needed'. So for example Quinton holds that if infinite justificatory regression is to be avoided, there must be a belief which, though indeed justified somehow, does not owe its justification to the support provided by others. And part of his reason for holding this is that 'for an inferential belief to be justified, the beliefs that support it must be justified themselves'.[1] Deutscher would agree. 'A person may have a reason for belief,' he writes, 'simply in that he holds another belief. He is thereby made rational in the first belief only if he is reasonable in believing the second.'[2] But other writers, and in particular Austin and Wittgenstein, seem rather to think that regresses of justification may terminate on reaching a point at which further justification is simply not needed. The stopping-point is either the believing of a proposition whose actual content makes justification unnecessary, or a believing somehow privileged to be unjustified by the circumstances in which it occurs.

If being justified in believing *p* is being assured of *p*'s truth, then no-need doctrines of justification may seem to clash with my claim in section (1) of the previous chapter, that you are liable to want radical assurance of the truth of every member of the essential core of your belief-system. For when radical assurance is evidential, it is ultra-regressive, and with ultra-regressive assurance every proposition you affirm to be evidence is a proposition of whose truth you are assured (see pp. 32–3 above). I must therefore ask whether Austin or Wittgenstein gives cogent arguments for the no-need doctrine in any version which really is incompatible with my thesis about our liability to want radical assurance.

I have already distinguished two species of no-need doctrine: one

[1] Quinton (1973) p. 119
[2] Deutscher (1973) p. 10

postulates particular propositions for the believing of which justification is not needed; the other particular circumstances in which justification is not needed for whatever is believed. A further division is enforced by the ambiguity of 'need'. What is needed is either an essential means of getting what is wanted, and thus *prima facie* something which is at least liable to be wanted, or it is something which it would be good to have. Using the two distinctions together, we arrive at the following four doctrines:

(A) There is a particular kind of proposition, distinguishable by its content, such that you are not liable, on reflecting about what you want of your belief-system as a whole, to be discontented at the thought that you affirm propositions of this kind to be evidence without having assured yourself of their truth

(B) There is a particular kind of circumstance, such that you are not liable, on reflecting about what you want of your belief-system as a whole, to be discontented at the thought that in circumstances of this kind you affirm propositions to be evidence without having assured yourself of their truth

(C) There is a particular kind of proposition, distinguishable by its content, such that it is just as good for you to affirm some proposition of this kind to be evidence without assuring yourself of its truth, as to have a belief-system in which you assure yourself of the truth of every proposition you affirm to be evidence

(D) There is a particular kind of circumstance such that it is just as good that in circumstances of this kind you affirm a proposition of this kind to be evidence without assuring yourself of its truth, as that you have a belief-system in which you assure yourself of the truth of every proposition you affirm to be evidence

Each of these doctrines has some relevance to my previous thesis that you are liable to want radical assurance of the truth of every member of the essential core of your belief-system. (A) and (B) are each incompatible with that thesis, if we assume that the unassured affirmations they refer to will be of propositions belonging to an essential core. And although neither (C) nor (D) is incompatible with my previous thesis, believing either (C) or (D) might give you some consolation for not being able to gain the radical assurance

which according to that thesis you are liable to want. Since I cannot
see that no-need theories of justification have any relevance to my
thesis about wanting radical assurance except when they entail one
or other of (A)–(D), I now ask which, if any, of (A)–(D) Austin
and Wittgenstein actually accepted, and what grounds, if any, they
give for thinking that any of (A)–(D) is true.

Austin thought that there is no particular kind of proposition,
distinguishable by content, which you always need evidence or
verification for, just as there is no particular kind of proposition,
distinguishable in that way, for which evidence or verification is
never needed. Whether or not you need evidence or verification
depended for him not on what proposition you assert, but on the
circumstances in which you assert it. There can, he wrote, be no
'*general* answer to the questions what is evidence for what, what is
certain, what is doubtful, what needs or does not need evidence, can
or can't be verified'.[1] Sentences or propositions – 'as distinct from
statements made in particular circumstances – cannot be divided up
at all on these principles'.[2] 'It is . . . not true in general that statements about "material things", as such, *need* to be verified'.[3] 'If, for
instance, someone remarks in casual conversion, "As a matter of fact
I live in Oxford", the other party to the conversation may, if he
finds it worth doing, verify this assertion; but the *speaker*, of course,
has no need to do this – he knows it to be true (or, if he is lying,
false).'[4] So if Austin would have accepted any of (A)–(D), it would
have been either (B) or (D). But actually, he was not at all concerned
with the assurance you are likely to want if you reflect about what
you want of your belief-system as a whole, but rather with the
assurance you are likely to want in the ordinary situations of daily
life. Since scepticism is nothing more than the wilful misdescription
of everyday questions and answers, eliminable by a self-conscious
return to naivety, there is no point in considering what happens
when someone views his belief-system as a whole. In some ordinary
circumstances of daily life you assert a proposition without wanting
anything else to which verification of that proposition would be a
means, so you do not need verification for it. In some ordinary
circumstances of daily life you know the proposition you assert

[1] Austin (1962) p. 124
[2] ibid. p. 123
[3] ibid. p. 117
[4] ibid. pp. 117–18

without having evidence for it, so you do not need evidence for it in order to know it. The sceptic about radical assurance will be undisturbed by these reminders because he is not talking either about the ordinary circumstances of daily life or about the conditions of knowledge.

Wittgenstein, on the other hand, might easily have rejected something like (A) and accepted something like (C). ((A) was that there is a particular kind of proposition, distinguishable by its content, such that you are not liable on reflecting about what you want of your belief-system as a whole, to be discontented at the thought that you affirm propositions of this kind to be evidence without having assured yourself of their truth. And (C) was that there is a particular kind of proposition, distinguishable by its content, such that it is just as good for you to affirm some proposition of this kind to be evidence without assuring yourself of its truth, as to have a belief-system in which you assure yourself of the truth of every proposition you affirm to be evidence.) In his remarks in *On Certainty*, he claims that there are propositions, which 'form the foundation of all operating with thoughts',[1] and which we do not arrive at as the result of investigations or even 'see' to be true. That I have two hands, for instance, or that the earth has existed during the last hundred years. And 'If I say "*we assume* that the earth has existed for many years past" (or something similar), then of course it sounds strange that we should *assume* such a thing'.[2] We are then liable, on reflexion, to want assurance of the truth of those propositions in the unassured believing of which we actually do end our regresses of assurance. Wittgenstein's aim is not to deny this but to reconcile us to the unavailability of this assurance, the strangeness of simply *assuming*, by a further series of reflexions: 'it sounds strange that we should *assume* such a thing. But in the entire system of language-games it belongs to the foundations. The assumption, one might say, forms the basis of action, and, therefore, naturally, of thought'.[3] The difficulty is to understand how this differs from the stoical thought more blandly expressed by Hume. But it does at any rate seem clear that there is nothing in Wittgenstein's version of the no-need theory of justification which is incompatible with my thesis about our

[1] Wittgenstein (1969) section 401
[2] ibid. section 411
[3] ibid.

liability to want radical assurance. I will come back to Humean and other consolations for scepticism in Chapter 8.

I began this section by contrasting the no-need doctrine of justification with the view that you cannot be inferentially justified or reasonable in believing p unless you are also justified or reasonable in believing the proposition which you believe to be evidence for p. But some philosophers have denied, not that you must be justified or reasonable in believing the proposition which you believe to be evidence for p but rather that you must be justified or reasonable in believing the proposition that this proposition is evidence for p. I am thinking in particular of Braithwaite, in the discussion of induction in Chapter 8 of his *Scientific Explanation*. Radical assurance is ultra-regressive when evidential, and with ultra-regressive assurance every proposition you affirm to be evidence is a proposition which you are assured *is* evidence. It may therefore be as well to look briefly at Braithwaite's arguments.

Braithwaite is concerned with the question of how it is possible to be reasonable in accepting the general effectiveness of a policy of concluding from past observations that something is true of the unobserved. And in particular he is concerned with the question of whether it is possible to become reasonable in accepting the general effectiveness of an inductive policy by inference from the proposition, which one is reasonable in accepting, that this policy has been effective in the past. He assumes that this inference would itself have to be made in accordance with the inductive policy whose general effectiveness one was hoping to become reasonable in accepting, but points out that this would only make the inference illegitimate if it were a necessary condition for the legitimacy of an inference that one was reasonable in accepting the general effectiveness of the policy in accordance with which the inference was made, and not a sufficient condition that this policy was in fact generally effective, or that one believed that this policy was generally effective. He then goes on to argue that the requirement that we must be reasonable in accepting the general effectiveness of the inferential policy would invalidate the majority of the inferences we actually make, including deductive inferences.

[The requirement that] to obtain a reasonable belief by inference ... we must have reasonable belief all along the line, reasonable belief in the effectiveness of the policy of inference no less than reasonable belief in the premiss ... would admit only deductions in which the proposition authenticating the principle of inference used was either seen directly to be true or was seen directly to be a logical consequence (in a chain of proof sufficiently short to be taken in at one glance) of a proposition seen directly to be true. Any other way of attaining belief in the effectiveness of the policy of deduction, e.g. by citing authority, or by remembering that one had satisfied oneself of its truth in the past, would involve inductive steps, and would thus not permit the belief to be 'reasonable', since the inference by which it had been obtained, or upon which it could be based, would not satisfy this stringent condition for validity.[1]

A difficulty with this argument is to see why, in the case of a deductive inference, belief in the effectiveness of the principle of inference used could be obtained only if 'the proposition authenticating the principle ... was either seen directly to be true or was seen directly to be a logical consequence (in a chain of proof sufficiently short to be taken in at one glance) of a proposition seen directly to be true'. Why should the mental activity which gives me assurance that q is deductive evidence for p not be spread over a longer period than this? If I cite evidence for the activity's having taken place, this may have to be inductive evidence; and there may be special difficulties about assuring oneself that one proposition is inductive evidence for another. But why should it be necessary, in order to be assured that q is inductive evidence for p, that one has assured oneself that one is assured?

Braithwaite supplements this argument with an ethical analogy

we think that a man is acting rightly if he does what he believes to be the objectively right action, irrespective of whether or not this belief of his is a reasonable one. If we think that his belief is an unreasonable one, and that he might, for example, by a previous more diligent study of the facts of the situation, have prevented himself from having this unreasonable belief, and instead acquired a different and reasonable belief, we may blame him for his past sin of omission in not having taken the steps he might have taken to acquire a more reasonable belief. But we do not blame him for his present belief, whether this be reasonable or unreasonable. Similarly, we should consider a man reasonable in following an

[1] Braithwaite (1953) pp. 283–4

inductive policy which he believed to be effective, independently of whether or not his belief was a reasonable one.[1]

But I think it is fairly clear that this discussion of blame-worthiness has no bearing on what sort of assurance we are actually liable to want, and in fact just illustrates the obstructive ambiguity of our ordinary usage of 'reasonable belief' (cf. p. 8 above). Suppose you really are prepared to approve of, or not condemn, my inferring p from q provided only that I believe that q is evidence for p and even if I would not have believed this if I had conducted a more careful investigation into whether it really is evidence. It certainly does not follow that in believing p on the basis of this inference I do not want to be assured that q really is evidence for p, or that you would not want to be assured of this if you were in my place. Questions about whether it is better to praise or blame a man for believing something, or for the previous activity or inactivity without which he would not have had the belief, are quite different from questions about which activities of investigation people are liable to want their believings to be contingent upon. It is perfectly possible to be liable to want ultra-regressive evidential assurance, and yet not think either that having it is good, or that there is anything blameworthy about the most deliberate failure to achieve it.

(2) *Self-justification and justification by experience*

Writers who offer a terminus for the regress of justification and accept that you cannot be inferentially justified in believing p unless you are also justified in believing the proposition which you take to be evidence for p offer us either beliefs justified by experience or beliefs which justify themselves. How do these two doctrines relate to my thesis about our liability to want radical assurance?

The first step must be to ask what 'justification' actually means, in 'justification by experience'. Is being justified by experience in believing p a matter simply of believing p in experiential circumstances such that the proposition that one believes p in these circumstances is evidence for p's truth? Or is it a matter of actually *assuring* oneself that p is true by an investigation which terminates in having an experience? Neither interpretation fits the most prominent texts; and yet at the same time it seems in these texts as though

[1] Braithwaite (1953) p. 287

the relations between experience and the proposition whose believing it is supposed to justify, or between the experience and the believing it is supposed to justify, are tacitly endowed with features which cannot really be possessed by anything but relations between propositions or between the believing of a proposition and conscious thought about its truth-value. Quinton's recent treatment of justification by experience is I think a case in point. He holds it a condition for you to understand the meaning of certain types of sentence that when experience prompts you to use a sentence of one of these types to assert a proposition about the experience, then that proposition is at least probably true, and the prompting experience justifies you in believing it. He also holds that when experience justifies you in believing a proposition, that proposition has 'experiential probability', a probability which, though relational, is not 'a relation to a belief, to other statements, is (not) propositional in nature'.[1]

> If a man who, looking into a room, says 'there's a fire in here', is asked if he has any evidence for saying so, when he has in fact seen the fire, although he might feel that the question was a bit cumbrously expressed in the circumstances, it would be ridiculous for him to answer 'no'. The proper answer would be 'Yes, I can see it'. (For him to do so is for him to say that the circumstances are sufficient to justify his assertion experientially, not to state his propositional evidence for it.)[2]

Whatever we think of Quinton's general doctrine about the connexion between the meaning of sentences and the probable truth of experiential propositions (I will come back to this in section (2) of Chapter 5), there does seem to be something unnecessarily paradoxical about the notions of 'experiential probability', and 'non-propositional evidence'. Why can we not say that what makes a proposition justified by experience probable is not its relation to 'non-propositional evidence' but rather its relation to a proposition to the effect that (a) an experience occurred, and (b) if it was not that usually when an experience like that prompts a man to assert a proposition he says something true, then he could not have learned the meaning of the sort of sentence he used to express the proposition? If the man really is asked for *evidence* that there is a fire, he can

[1] Quinton (1973) p. 160
[2] ibid. pp. 209–10

reply either by saying that it looks to him as if there is one, or by
saying that experience prompted him to say there was one and then
rehearsing Quinton's general doctrine about understanding the
meaning of sentences and the probable truth of experiential propositions. In either case he would be citing propositional evidence. ('I
can see it' would on the other hand be a good answer to 'How do
you know there is a fire in there?') Another advocate of justification
by experience, Max Deutscher, goes so far as to claim that the mere
having of an experience can make one 'reasonable' in believing a
proposition; a man is reasonable in holding a belief only if either he
holds it for a reason or reasons, or if he has a 'ground' for holding
it. One has a ground for believing that one has a headache if one
feels it. To have a ground is not to have a belief.[1] Having a ground
can not only make a man reasonable in believing something, it can
justify him in his own belief, if x believes that y committed the
crime, and actually watched him do it, 'his direct observation of the
crime makes him reasonable or justifies him in his own belief'.[2]

The idiom comes, I suspect, from a too hasty effort to reconcile
the existence of non-inferential knowledge with the classical theory
that N knows that p only if p is true and he is justified in believing
that p. It is assumed that since an infinite regress of justification
would be vicious, some empirical knowledge must be non-inferential if anyone has any empirical knowledge at all. Since scepticism is
'absurdly defeatist' (Quinton), and N knows that p only if he is
justified in believing that p, and no proposition entailing the existence of a concrete object can be validated by the pure light of reason,
it must be possible for N to be justified in accepting such a proposition simply by having an experience. But what does 'N is justified in
believing p' actually mean, in the classical theory of knowledge?
More, clearly, than 'N believes p and p is at least probably true'. The
problem is to show that it does not mean too much more for 'N is
justified in believing p by having an experience' to mean anything at
all.

But however this may be, no doctrine of justification by experience will threaten my thesis about our liability to want radical
assurance unless it says either that we are not liable to be discontented at the prospect that some of our regresses of assurance should
terminate in believings justified only in the sense that what is

[1] Deutscher (1973) p. 11
[2] ibid. p. 9

believed is at least probably true, or that we are not liable to be discontented at the prospect that some of our regresses of assurance
should terminate in a purely sensory assurance of truth.

We can apply this dilemma even to those terminologically careful
writers, like Ayer, for whom having an experience does not necessarily either give one evidence or make one reasonable, but only
gives one 'the right to be sure'.[1] Is the right to be sure that *p* auto-
matically conferred on you whenever *p* is both believed by you and
at least probably true? Or is it a right which you have consciously
done something to earn? It does at all events seem to me quite plainly
true that if you once consider the matter you will want active assurance of the truth of what you affirm to be evidence, and not just a
right to be sure which you may not in any particular case even know
that you possess. And it is also true, though less obviously, that you
are liable to want more than sensory assurance of the truth of what
you affirm to be evidence. The point here is that you are liable to
want both assurance and consciousness of the nature of the activity
by which you have gained it. And as I have already argued, the two
are compatible only when assurance is either evidential or intuitive
(see pp. 21–2 above).

I also referred at the beginning of this section to the idea that a
regress of justification can be terminated by self-justifying beliefs.
With this I can now be fairly brief. If an infinite regress of justification is to be vicious it must be a regress of assurance. It is not clear
that a man cannot believe each member of an infinite series of different propositions; and if he can, there is no reason why each one
should not be both true or probably true and succeeded in the series
by another proposition which is evidence for its truth. It is only on
an active interpretation of justification, only if being justified in
believing something requires an activity of investigation, that there
is anything clearly vicious about an infinite regress of justification.[2]
But now, a regress of assurance can terminate only in someone's
believing a proposition. By a 'self-justifying belief' you may mean
either a self-justifying proposition or a self-justifying state of believing. Propositions can be self-justifying in the sense of self-evident,
capable of being metaphorically seen to be true. And believings can
be self-justifying in the sense that there are values of *p* such that '*N*
believes *p*' entails '*p* or probably *p*'. But believings cannot be self-

[1] Ayer (1969) p. 121
[2] cf. Alston (1976a) p. 173 n. 10

assuring; there are no values of *p* such that '*N* believes *p*' entails '*N* has assured himself that *p*'. So there is no interpretation of 'self-justifying belief' on which self-justifying beliefs are both existent and capable of terminating the kind of justificatory regress which infinity vitiates.

(3) *Foundationalism and coherence*

Regressive difficulties eliminate *a*-assurance, and therefore prevent us from having as much radical assurance as we are liable to want. But this is a version of the well-known doctrine that for much of what we believe, an infinite regress of justification is both necessary and impossible. And since current epistemology has proved that this doctrine is for one reason or other false, it will surely somehow also contain some answer to scepticism about radical assurance. So far, in my efforts to combat this objection, I have considered those current theories which, while conceding that a regress of justification cannot be infinite, claim that it is easily enough terminable in various kinds of basic propositions, believings or circumstances of belief. And by scrutiny of the actual meaning they attach to 'justification', 'not needed', etc., I have tried to show that these theories are either false or compatible with the thesis that extensive radical assurance is something we are liable to want. In the remaining two sections of this chapter I consider some theories on which justificatory regression is either allowably infinite, or not even allowed to begin.

An often attempted dichotomy would give us on the one hand *coherence* and on the other hand *foundations* or *linear* theories of justification or knowledge. And the suspicion is current that sceptical difficulties about justificatory regression stem from foundationalist preconceptions and a consequent failure to grasp the role of coherence in justified believing. 'If we suppose that beliefs are to be justified by deducing them from more basic beliefs,' writes Harman, 'we will suppose that there are beliefs so basic that they cannot be justified at all. To avoid the conclusion that these must be taken on faith, we may suggest that they can be seen to be true by direct and immediate intuition, perhaps by virtue of our knowledge of the language.' The conclusion cannot really be avoided in this way, Harman thinks, because there is in the end nothing to choose between the appeal to analyticity, the appeal to the natural light of reason and the appeal to magic. Things change, however, with the adoption of a coherence theory of justification. 'These sceptical views are undermined (or at least take different forms) once it is seen that the relevant kind of justification is not a matter of derivation from basic principles but is rather a matter of showing that a view fits in well with other things we believe.'[1] Or, as an even more recent writer puts it, 'foundationism appears to be doomed by its own internal momentum. No account seems to be available of how an empirical belief can be genuinely justified in an epistemic sense, while avoiding all reference to further empirical beliefs or cognitions which themselves would require justification. How then is the epistemic regress problem to be solved? The natural direction to look for an answer is to the coherence theory of empirical knowledge and the associated non-linear conception of justification.'[2]

But what exactly *is* a foundational theory of justification? Presumably, it is some thesis to the effect that if there is any proposition p which you are justified in believing only because you are justified in believing some other proposition then there is some proposition evidentially related to p or believed by you to be so related, which you are either not justified in believing or justified in believing in a way which does not require you to be justified in believing something else. But of course whether a thesis of this kind is true, or one to which I am committed by scepticism about radical assurance, depends on how 'justification' is interpreted. And I also think that, ambiguous though 'justification' is in current philosophical usage (see pp. 38–42 above), there is *no* usual sense of the term on which 'foundations theory of justification' and 'coherence theory of justification' are apt and convenient labels for a pair of mutually exclusive propositions. So even if my scepticism about radical assurance does commit me to a foundational theory of justification, there may easily also be some true and aptly named coherence theory of justification, in that or another sense of 'justification', which consistency permits or even requires me to accept.

Suppose we interpret 'N is justified in believing p' non-actively, i.e. as not entailing that N has conducted any conscious and deliberate investigation into the truth-value of p. It might, compatibly with this, entail, in addition to 'N believes p', one or more of the following propositions (i) 'p is true or probably true'; (ii) 'There is a non-coincidental connexion between p's being true or probably true and

[1] Harman (1973) p. 164
[2] Bonjour (1978) p. 13

the circumstances in which N believes p', (iii) 'N believes a proposition q which is evidence for p; and believes that q is evidence for p'; (iv) 'If N is justified in believing one proposition only because he believes that a second proposition is evidence for it then he is justified in believing the second proposition and justified in believing that it is evidence for the first proposition'; (v) 'Given any particular member of the various infinite series of evidentially related propositions which permit the satisfaction of (iii) and (iv), N is able consciously and deliberately to assure himself that that member is true'. If 'justification' is interpreted in one or other of these non-active ways, then a foundations theory of justification is I think probably false. A foundations theory of justification says that if there is any proposition p which you are justified in believing only because you are justified in believing some other proposition then there is some proposition evidentially related to p or believed to be so related, which you are either not justified in believing, or justified in believing in a way which does not require you to be justified in believing something else. A thesis of this kind will be true only if there is something vicious about an infinite regress of justification, and with 'justification' non-actively defined it is not clear that such a regress is impossible (see p. 99 above). But it does not follow from the falsity of a foundational theory of non-active justification, that anything which it is at all natural to call a coherence theory of justification is true. A coherence theory might say that what justifies you in believing p is that p belongs, or is believed by you to belong, to some kind of coherent set of propositions. Alternatively, it might say that you can be justified in believing p by being justified in believing q, justified in believing q by being justified in believing $q_1, \ldots,$ justified in believing q_{n-1} by being justified in believing q_n, and justified in believing q_n by being justified in believing a member of the set $\{p, q, q_1, \ldots, q_{n-1}\}$; 'the regress of justification $\ldots$ circles back upon itself'.[2] Neither of these doctrines follows from the denial of a foundations theory, when 'justification' is taken in a non-active sense.

What then if we take 'justification' in an active sense, so that 'N is justified in believing p' entails that N has consciously and deliberately investigated p's truth-value, assured himself that p? If we build stringent conditions for evidential assurance into an active concept of justification, require for example that you must always

[1] Bonjour (1976) p. 283

assure yourself of the truth of any proposition you cite as evidence, then it follows, by the arguments of Chapter 2, that a foundational theory of justification is true. And certainly, if justification is radical assurance, then I am committed to a foundations theory of justification. But this does not mean that I must deny everything it would be natural to call a coherence theory, on that same interpretation of 'justification'. I must deny that you can be justified in believing p by being justified in believing q, justified in believing q by being justified in believing $q_1, \ldots$, justified in believing q_{n-1} by being justified in believing q_n, and justified in believing q_n by being justified in believing a member of the set $\{ p, q, q_1, \ldots, q_{n-1} \}$. But I do not have to deny that for gaining evidential assurance of p's truth, the only admissible evidence is that p belongs to a set of propositions with explanatory or some other kind of coherence.

Given the ambiguity of 'justification', the best policy is I think to stop talking about foundational and coherence theories of justification, and use the foundations/coherence distinction to mark divisions among doctrines about some of the more specific things towards which so-called theories of justification ambiguously gesture. 'Coherence theory of evidence' might then simply be the name for such principles of evidence as: 'if p is contingent then q is evidence for p if q is to the effect that p belongs to a coherent set of propositions', and 'if p_1 and p_2 are contingent, q is evidence for "p_1 is more likely to be true than p_2" if q is to the effect that p_1 belongs to a coherent set of propositions and p_2 does not'. 'Foundations theory of evidence' might pick out the view that propositions can be exhaustively divided into two kinds such that no member of the first kind has any other proposition as evidence for it, and every member of the second kind is such that some member of the first kind is either evidence for it, or evidence for a proposition which is evidence for it, or ... etc. 'Foundations theory of assurance' might stand for the view that if a man is to have the sort of assurance of truth he is liable to want, then if there are any propositions of whose truth he is evidentially assured there will be some propositions of whose truth he is not evidentially assured, and which he affirms to be evidence for propositions of whose truth he is evidentially assured. And 'Coherence theory of assurance' might stand for the view that you can evidentially assure yourself that p, in the way you want to, by citing q as evidence for p and being evidentially assured that q_{n-1} by adducing q_n as evidence for it, and being evidentially assured that q_n by adducing as evidence for it one of the propositions in the set $\{p, q, q_1, \ldots, q_{n-1}\}$. Putting the matter in these terms, my theses about radical assurance require a foundations theory of assurance and rule out a coherence theory of assurance and a foundations theory of evidence, but neither rule out nor require a coherence theory of evidence.

It would I think also be useful to apply these distinctions to current epistemological writing of an ostensibly 'anti-foundationalist' and 'coherentist' cast. Rescher, for example, in his *Coherence Theory of Truth*, aims to construct a 'coherentist epistemology (which) stands in sharp contrast with the foundationalist approach of the mainstream tradition of western epistemology ... (and) dispenses with any appeal to basic, foundational truths of fact'.[1] Various rules are given for singling out propositions from sets of 'data' i.e. sets of propositions which 'taken individually ... are merely truth-presumptive, but taken collectively ... are truth-containing'.[2] And he shows that a proposition can be singled out from a set of data by one of these rules only if it belongs to what is in some sense a coherent sub-set of a set of data. If Rescher is claiming that it is evidence for a proposition that it can be singled out from a set of data by one of these rules, then he will be advancing what is in my terminology a coherence theory of evidence. But this does not in the least mean, as his own terminology might lead us to suppose, that he rejects a foundationalist theory of assurance. On the contrary, he accepts that version of a foundationalist theory of assurance on which the ultimate evidence for whose truth one has no evidential assurance is made up of propositions which one remembers or perceives to be true. For on the question of how we are to assure ourselves that a set of propositions *is* a set of data, he says only that data are provided by the senses, memory, etc., and that 'to rest discontent with this foundation of sensory knowledge on sceptical grounds because "the theoretical possibility of error" cannot be excluded totally is not to be *irrational* (i.e. in conflict with the demands of logic) but it is utterly unreasonable by imposing upon observational knowledge a condition which – by the very nature of the thing at issue – it is in principle incapable of meeting'.[3] Another defender of the coherence theory of empirical knowledge claims that there are

[1] Rescher (1973) pp. 317–18
[2] ibid. p. 57   [3] ibid. p. 331

two levels at which issues of justification can be raised ... the issue ... may be merely the justification of a particular belief, or a small set of beliefs, in the context of a cognitive system whose overall justification is taken for granted; or it may be the global issue of the justification of the cognitive system itself. According to the (coherence theory of empirical knowledge) it is the latter, global issue which is fundamental for the determination of epistemic justification ... At the level at which only the justification of a particular belief ... is at issue justification appears linear. A given justificandum belief is justified explicitly by citing other premise beliefs from which it may be inferred. Such premise-beliefs can themselves be challenged, with justification provided for them in the same fashion. But there is no serious chance of a regress at this level since the justification of the overall epistemic system (and thus of at least most of its component beliefs) is *ex hypothesi* not at issue. One thus quickly reaches premise beliefs which are dialectically acceptable in that context ... At this global level, however, the (coherence theory of empirical knowledge) no longer conceives the relation between the various particular beliefs as one of linear dependence, but rather as one of mutual or reciprocal support. There is no ultimate relation of epistemic priority among the members of such a system and consequently no basis for a true regress. The component beliefs are so related that each can be justified in terms of the others; the direction in which the justifying argument actually moves depends on which belief is under scrutiny in a particular context. The apparent circle of justification is not vicious because the justification of particular beliefs depends finally not on other particular beliefs, as in the linear conception of justification, but on the overall system and its coherence.[1]

I suspect that in talking of what it is for a belief to be justified at the local level, the author is talking of the sort of assurance a man is liable to want, and in talking of what it is for a belief to be justified at the global level he is talking of what is evidence for the proposition believed. We are content, in everyday circumstances, to halt a regress of assurance in unassured affirmation, in something 'dialectically acceptable'. It is evidence for a proposition that it belongs to a 'coherent overall system', or at any rate to a coherent overall system

[1] Bonjour (1976) pp. 286–7

which has what the author subsequently refers to as 'input from the world'.[1] But are we content with unassured affirmation when we look at our belief-system from a global point of view? The 'coherence theory of empirical knowledge' is entirely compatible with a negative answer.

But even granting the general danger of tidy-looking dichotomies, and accepting the suggested re-classification of theories of evidence and assurance, you may still wonder whether pessimism about the scope of β-assurance is really compatible with a full appreciation of the potentialities of a coherence theory of evidence. Suppose we can somehow be β-assured that for any contingent proposition p, q is evidence for p when q is a proposition to the effect that p belongs to a certain sort of coherent set of propositions. Might there not be some unexpected way in which we can be β-assured that a contingent proposition belongs to this sort of coherent set? If so, then I will have underestimated the number of contingent propositions of whose truth we can gain β-assurance, and then, even if α-assurance is impossible, radical assurance will not be as hopelessly scarce as I have made it out to be.

To see whether there is anything in this suspicion, we must look more closely at coherence principles of evidence. Suppose there are two sets of propositions A and B such that every member of A is explained by one or more members of B, no member of A explains any member of B, and B provides what is in some sense the simplest explanation of A. The union of A and B could be usefully called a coherent set, and the principle that q is evidence for p if q is the proposition that p belongs to such a union could usefully be called a coherence principle of evidence. Is it a plausible principle? Surely not. It could very well be that, for most pairs of sets whose union satisfies these conditions for coherence, the explained set contains only false members, and in this case the proposition that p belongs to such a union would not be evidence for p's truth. Should we require then that the explained set contains all contingently true explicable but non-explanatory propositions? The coherence principle will still be false, if p is an explicable and non-explanatory proposition. For in this case 'q is evidence for p if q is the proposition that p belongs to a coherent set' will be equivalent to 'q is evidence for p if q is the proposition that p is a contingently true explicable and non-explanatory proposition', which makes the

[1] ibid. p. 289

argument 'q therefore p' question-begging. What we need is a way of picking out the explained set without saying simply that it is the set of all explicable and non-explanatory propositions which are contingently true. Suppose that all contingently true propositions are either ostensive in the sense of expressible by ostensively learned sentences, or parts of, or entailed by parts of, the simplest explanation of all true ostensive propositions. And suppose there is a consistent set of ostensive propositions A such that any subset of A which contains most or all of A's members contains most true ostensive propositions. Let B and C be sets of propositions such that B is a subset of A containing most or all of A's members, C contains nothing but explanations of B's members, and C explains B more simply than any other set of propositions which (i) explains any subset of A containing most or all of A's members, and (ii) contains nothing but explanations of that subset of A. The union of B and C will then form what it is again natural enough to call a coherent set, and we can formulate the coherence principle of evidence that if p is a contingent proposition and q the proposition that p belongs to the union of B and C then q is evidence for p. Another way of expressing the principle would be to say that q is evidence for p if it is to the effect that p belongs to a consistent set comprising most or all of A's members and also an explanation of these members and from which it is impossible to add or subtract without either (i) producing an inconsistent set, or (ii) producing a set which contains non-explanatory members which are not members of A, or (iii) producing a set which contains more complex explanations of a subset of A containing most or all of A's members. Some writers have suggested that it is a necessary condition for the existence of meaningful sentences that most of the ostensive propositions which experience actually prompts people to assert are true. Perhaps we can be β-assured that this principle is true. Perhaps we can also be β-assured that A, in our final coherence principle of evidence, can be identified with the set of ostensive propositions which experience prompts people to assert. And could we not then be β-assured about the truth-value of propositions to the effect that a particular contingent proposition belongs to A, and indeed to the union of B and C? And then, if we could also be β-assured of the truth of the final coherence principle of evidence itself, pessimism about the scope of β-assurance would be totally unfounded.

This is a popular train of thought and one which deserves detailed examination. But failure to appreciate its strength could just as well be called confusion over the conditions for the meaningfulness of sentences as failure to appreciate the potentialities of a coherence theory of evidence. And it will in fact be convenient to delay my scrutiny until chapter 5, where I can link it to the discussion of some other anti-sceptical arguments which invoke general doctrines about meaning. It is however worth noting a peculiarity of the coherence principle of evidence we were finally left with. You cannot actually *apply* this principle, in order to become radically and evidentially assured of a proposition's truth, unless you can be radically assured that certain particular ostensive propositions are ones which experience has prompted people to assert, and also radically assured that most such ostensive propositions are true. But in this case you do not need a coherence principle of evidence in order to become radically and evidentially assured of the truth of ostensive propositions. It seems that if a coherence principle of evidence is applicable at all, it is redundant over part of its range of application.

(4) *Critical Rationalism*

I will conclude this chapter by trying to banish the suspicion that my difficulties about the regressive character of radical and evidential assurance are somehow undermined by the discoveries of Critical Rationalism. Critical Rationalists suggest that we can in all circumstances be content with a rational believing which requires no more than that we have succeeded in meeting many serious objections to what we believe, and that there are no serious objections which we have not succeeded in meeting. Contrasts are drawn with epistemologies which postulate propositions simply 'seen' to be true or believings validated by the mere having of sensory experience: such doctrines escape from infinite justificatory regression only at the price of 'dogmatism' or 'psychologism' or even 'authoritarianism'. Contrasts are drawn also with the primitive and hopeless quest for certainty or absolute security of belief. All these errors and pitfalls can be avoided if we abandon 'justificationism' and content ourselves with an essentially critical or negative form of rationality.[1] Is it not then precisely a form of 'justificationism' which I have in effect been defending?

[1] Bartley (1964) pp. 139–46; Albert (1969) pp. 29–37

If Critical Rationalists were saying only that it is all right to believe anything unless you are presented with an objection to it which you are unable to meet, then it would be clear at any rate that a proposition does not have to be even probably true in order for you to be critically rational in believing it. But what they actually say is that it is *not* all right to believe a proposition *unless* many objections to it have been put forward and disposed of. And the point of insisting on this condition is presumably to ensure that what we believe is at least probably true. But (a) if critical rationality guarantees the truth or probable truth of what is rationally believed, then difficulties of infinite regression supervene, and (b) it is in any case self-contradictory to suppose that critical rationality does guarantee this truth or probable truth.

(a) Consider the Critical Rationalist's notion of meeting an objection to *p*. Is it supposed to be sufficient for *N* to have met an objection to *p* that there is some false or probably false proposition *q*, whose truth would be difficult to reconcile with *p*'s truth, and which *N* believes to be false? Or is it necessary that he is in some sense *rational* in believing *q* to be false? Presumably the latter, if meeting an objection is more than a merely accidental advance towards the truth. But then what *is* the sense in which *N* must be rational in believing *q*'s falsity? Presumably, he has to be *critically* rational in believing *q*'s falsity. But in this case *N* will not be rational in believing that *q* is false unless many serious objections have been made against *q*'s falsity and he has met all of them. So there will have to be a further proposition *r*, whose truth would be difficult to reconcile with *q*'s falsity, and which *N* is critically rational in believing to be false, and hence a further proposition *s*, whose truth would be difficult to reconcile with *r*'s falsity, and which *N* is critically rational in believing to be false, and so on ad infinitum. So it seems impossible to be critically rational in believing any proposition without being critically rational in believing each member of an infinite series of propositions. Is this something which anyone has time for? As I pointed out in Chapter 2, there is no actual contradiction in supposing that someone should find the time. But the supposition would be consistent only if rather special conditions were satisfied by the relative durations of the objection-meeting operations (see pp. 57–8 above). And it is hard to see how exactly the critical dialectic would go with the proposition that these conditions are sometimes satisfied. (Critical Rationalists do not themselves say exactly why they think an infinite regress of justification vicious.)

(b) To see why it is self-contradictory to suppose that critical rationality guarantees truth or probable truth, imagine that, although *N* has met all the many serious objections which have been made against some proposition *p* which he believes, he has also met all the many serious objections which have been made against *not-p*. Then according to the Critical Rationalist he would be rational in believing *p* and also rational in believing *not-p*. But if a man's being rational in believing something is supposed to guarantee that what he believes is true or probably true, it follows that *p* and *not-p* are both either true or probably true, which is absurd.

The consistent Critical Rationalist will of course reply that no such case can arise, since the very fact that one has succeeded in meeting many serious objections to *p* constitutes a serious and unmet objection to *not-p*. The fact that one has met the objections to *p* makes *p* probably true and therefore makes *not-p* probably false. But might not one's success in meeting objections to *p* be equally well accounted for in terms of the objector's incapacities? Would you for example really be prepared to say that, simply by refuting a series of impressive-looking materialist arguments, you have demonstrated the probable existence of an immaterial substance?

Perhaps the Critical Rationalist concept can be modified: you are rational in believing *p* if and only if (i) many serious objections have been made against *p* and you have met them all, and (ii) it is not the case that many serious objections have been made against *not-p* and you have met them all. But this leads to difficulties. Suppose you have met all of many serious objections to immaterialism. Then the Critical Rationalist would have to say that you are not rational in believing that there is a spiritual substance unless either not many serious objections have been made against materialism or of the many serious objections against materialism which have been made, there are some you have not met. But an objection against materialism is an argument for immaterialism. So the Critical Rationalist must say that you are not rational in believing that there is a spiritual substance unless there are not many arguments for immaterialism, or you have an argument for immaterialism which you cannot see anything wrong with. The first requirement seems paradoxical, and reliance on the second deprives Critical Rationalism of any separate identity: its whole special contribution to the theory of rationality was supposed to lie in the substitution of survival under bombard-ment for positive argument.

In a way, this is hardly a surprising result. The notion of critical rationality is derived from Popper's *Logik der Forschung* rules for the 'game of science', the game of 'acceptance', 'falsification' and 'corroboration'. And these rules were not designed for the pursuit of truth or even meant to regulate anything properly describable as *believing*. To 'accept' a theory, in the sense of that book, is not to believe that it is true, for a theory to be 'falsified' is not for it to be false, and for it to be relatively well 'corroborated' is not for it to be any more likely to be true or less likely to be false. For a theory to be relatively well corroborated is for there to have been relatively many unsuccessful attempts to falsify it and no successful attempts. For a theory to be falsified is for it to be known that it stands in certain logical relationships with basic propositions which are convention-ally agreed to be true. A proposition is basic if (i) it is a singular existential proposition of the form 'There is an x at time t, place p'; (ii) it reports the occurrence of an event which is observable in the sense that it involves the position and movement of macroscopic physical bodies.[1] It is not sufficient for a theory to be falsified that there are basic propositions conventionally agreed to be true with which it is known to be incompatible. 'We shall take it as falsified only if we discover a *reproducible effect* which refutes the theory. In other words, we only accept the falsification if a low-level empirical hypothesis which describes such an effect is proposed and corroborated' – i.e. has passed tests which confront it with accepted basic statements.[2] For a theory to be accepted is simply for it to be decided that attempts to falsify it, or further attempts to falsify it, should be made. The relative acceptability of a theory is propor-tional to its degree of corroboration and to its content, i.e. to the number of different basic propositions, liable to be conventionally agreed to be true, with which it is incompatible. The acceptance of a theory is a rational matter only in the sense that there are acceptance-rules which theories can satisfy and which we can work out whether they do satisfy. 'Our science is not knowledge (episteme): it can never claim to have attained truth, or even a substitute for it, such as probability.'[3] 'With the idol of certainty (including that of degrees

[1] Popper (1959) pp. 100–3
[2] ibid. pp. 86–7
[3] ibid. p. 278

of imperfect certainty or probability) there falls one of the defences of obscurantism which bars the way of scientific advance, checking the boldness of our questions, and endangering the rigour and integrity of our tests.'[1] It is too much to say, as Lakatos does, that 'there is nothing in the *Logik der Forschung* with which the most radical sceptic need disagree'.[2] Certain truths about logical relations have to be known, if the rules of the game are to be applied. And Popper also seems to imply that we can know which basic propositions people actually agree to accept. But it would of course be easy enough to say that a player is to count a theory as falsified if he knows that it stands in logical relations, of the sort described by Popper, to basic propositions which he merely believes that other players believe.

It is, of course, understandable enough that Critical Rationalists should have hesitated over a sceptical interpretation of the *Logik der Forschung*. For one thing, it is difficult to see how anyone could find scepticism as utterly undisturbing as Popper seems there to do. 'It is not his *possession* of knowledge, of irrefutable truth, that makes the man of science, but his persistent and recklessly critical *quest* for truth.'[3] And of course we have to understand that the man of science can never possess probable truth either. 'Den lieb' ich, der Unmögliches begehrt.' So totally?

There is some mystery also in Popper's claim to have resolved the Friesian Trilemma, the supposed choice between dogmatism, infinite regress and psychologism.

> The basic statements at which we stop, which we decide to accept as satisfactory, and as sufficiently tested, have admittedly the character of *dogmas* but only insofar as we may desist from justifying them by further arguments (or further tests). But this kind of dogmatism is innocuous since, should the need arise, these statements can easily be tested further. I admit that this too makes the chain of deduction infinite. But this kind of *'infinite regress'* is also innocuous since in our theory there is no question of trying to prove any statement by means of it.[4]

If the man of science has no knowledge, if the idol of knowledge is a defence of obscurantism, if it really is true that we have no knowledge of basic statements, and hence no knowledge of the falsity of

---

[1] ibid. pp. 280–1   [2] Lakatos (1974) p. 254
[3] Popper (1959) p. 281   [4] ibid. p. 105

any theory which they, metaphorically speaking, 'falsify', then why is it even *necessary* to try to show that dogmatism about basic statements is innocuous because such statements can always be tested further?

And finally, there is a certain lack of explicitness in Popper about the relation between his *Logik der Forschung* apparatus and his subsequent attitude to scepticism. His original sceptical leanings were a reaction to problems which he believes to have been subsequently solved by Tarski's theory of truth. 'Our falsifications,' he was later prepared to say, 'indicate the points where we have touched reality'.[1] More recently, justification itself has been at least partially reinstated:

> We can never rationally justify a theory – that is a claim to know its truth – but we can, if we are lucky, rationally justify a preference for one theory out of a set of competing theories, for the time being; that is, with respect to the present state of the discussion. And our justification, though not a claim that the theory is true, can be the claim that there is every indication at this stage of the discussion that the theory is *a better approximation to the truth* than any competing theory so far proposed.[2]

As Lakatos remarks, Popper has not fully exploited 'the possibilities opened up by his Tarskian turn'.[3] The obfuscating influence of this failure is illustrated by a reversal in Lakatos's own views. 'Popperian *critical fallibilism* takes the infinite regress in proofs and definitions seriously', he wrote in 1962,

> (it) does not have illusions about stopping them, accepts the sceptic criticism of any infallible truth-injection . . . We never know, we only guess. We can, however, turn our guesses into critical ones, and criticise and improve them. In this Critical Programme, many of the old problems – like those of probabilities, induction, reduction, justification of *synthetic a priori*, justification of sense-experience, and so on – become pseudo-problems, since they all answer the wrong dogmatist question *How do you know?* Instead of these old problems, however, many new problems emerge. The new central question, *How do you improve your*

[1] Popper (1963) p. 116
[2] Popper (1972) p. 82
[3] Lakatos (1974) p. 256

guesses? will give enough work for philosophers for centuries; and how to live, act, fight, die when one is left with guesses only, will give more than enough work for future political philosophers and educationalists.[1]

But now we are to accept a 'principle of induction' which says that 'the methodology of scientific research programmes is better suited for approximating the truth in our actual universe than any other methodology . . . By refusing to accept this "thin metaphysical principle of induction" Popper fails to separate rationalism from irrationalism, weak light from total darkness. Without this principle Popper's "corroboration" or "refutations" and any "progress" and "degeneration", would remain mere honorific titles awarded in a pure game. With a *positive* solution to the problem of induction, however thin, methodological theories of demarcation can be turned from arbitrary conventions into rational metaphysics.'[2]

[1] Lakatos (1962) p. 165
[2] Lakatos (1974) p. 261

5

Self-evidence and self-defeat

In Chapter 3 I showed that radical assurance is something we are liable to want. And in the previous chapter I showed that my theses about our desire for radical assurance are not threatened by various current doctrines about how to terminate or circumvent an infinite regress of justification. In this present chapter I reconsider the actual availability of radical assurance. The position we reached on this point was that radical and β-assurance have a co-extensive scope (Chapter 2), and that the scope of β-assurance is very severely restricted by the plausible assumptions about self-evidence which I initially set out (Chapter 1, section (5)). N is β-assured that p, you will remember, if and only if he is radically assured that p and either (a) he is intuitively assured that p, or (b) there is a proposition of whose truth he is intuitively assured and which he believes to be overriding evidence, either for p, or for a proposition which he believes to be overriding evidence for a proposition which he believes to be overriding evidence for p, or . . ., and so on (see p. 48 above). One cannot be radically and intuitively assured that p unless p is self-evident (see p. 45 above), and a proposition is self-evident, on my initial assumptions, only if it does not entail the existence of any concrete entity other than a single subject of consciousness, and does not entail that someone is in any particular mental state or possesses any particular mental power other than the state or power of being conscious (see p. 45 above). What we now need to make sure of it that my assumptions about self-evidence really do limit the scope of β-assurance as severely as it initially seems, and that there is not some argument which, with the aid perhaps of a few minor and independently attractive modifications to these assumptions, will unexpectedly expand the scope of β-assurance, and expand it sufficiently for us to be no longer disturbed that radical and β-assurance have a co-extensive scope.

The most likely source of such an argument is in what we might call the standard dialectic of self-defeat. If no proposition is true, then neither is this universal hypothesis about truth. If there is no proposition whose truth-value is knowable then this universal thesis about knowledge, though maybe true, is nevertheless not knowable. What if the sceptic says only that there is no contingent proposition whose truth-value is knowable? If this restricted scepticism about knowledge were a contingent hypothesis, then it too would entail its own unknowability. Suppose then that the sceptic about knowledge of contingencies denies the contingency of his own hypothesis. This time there is a danger of self-defeat through self-trivialisation. If scepticism about our knowledge of contingencies is not to be trivial there must actually be some contingent propositions whose truth-value is knowable. But how can we know that there really is anything by virtue of which what a sentence expresses is true or false, if we cannot know the truth-value of what it expresses? Other arguments threaten, of a not openly verificationist kind. Surely the sceptical hypothesis is false, if intelligible at all, because if any sentence has a sense then there are at least some contingent propositions which we can know. For surely, if any sentence has a sense then some types of sentence will have been introduced into my language ostensively, and how can I not know that the propositions expressed by these ostensively introduced sentence-types are at least probably true? Or again, is it not necessary for my language to be public in order for the sentences in it to have a sense? If so, how can I not know those contingent propositions about the existence of other people or objects which are entailed by its public character? Alternatively, the sceptical hypothesis is false if accepted because if any proposition is believed then at least some contingent propositions are knowable. Possibly these contingent propositions amount to no more than a few bare Cartesian generalities about the existence and mental capacities of the believer himself. But possibly the harvest is richer, as Kant suggests: we can know that the believer is himself part of a lawfully changing plurality of objects. The question is whether any of these familiar thoughts on the self-defeating character of traditional scepticisms about truth and knowledge be adapted to show that there is something self-defeating in pessimism about the scope of β-assurance.

(1) *Verificationism and the idea of a predicate*

According to verificationism, it is a necessary condition for a sentence to be meaningful that we can have knowledge, or justified belief, or rational belief, or at any rate some sort of assurance, either that what it expresses is true, or that what it expresses is false. You can be a verificationist in this general sense without being committed to the logical positivist theory of meaning. The logical positivists held that a sentence is not meaningful unless what it expresses is either logically or analytically true or stands in a certain logical relation to an 'observation statement'. An observation statement was variously conceived of as a proposition made true or false or probably true or false purely by the occurrence or non-occurrence of some sensory experience, or as a proposition such that if it were true we would have the power to know it purely by sense-experience, and if it were false we would have the power similarly to know its negation. Someone who denied that it is sufficient for it to be meaningful either that what it expresses is made true by sense-experience, or that what it expresses is knowable by experience, might easily think it necessary for a sentence to be meaningful that we can be assured of the truth-value of what it expresses. And this would be enough to make him a verificationist in the generic sense. Nor of course does generic verificationism entail that the non-logical and non-analytical truths expressed by meaningful sentences are related to propositions entailing the occurrence of sensory experiences in anything like the ways that the logical positivists tried unsuccessfully to formulate.[1]

In order actually to apply any form of verificationism, one needs a distinction between things which are both expressed by sentences and either true or false, and things which are expressed by sentences but neither true nor false. When the verificationist talks of the conditions for a sentence to be meaningful, he means the conditions for it to express something either true or false. It would not be possible for him to find out whether a sentence expressed something true or false unless he could begin by considering what it expressed, and it would not be necessary for him to go any further unless it were possible for what it expressed not to meet his requirements. Ayer's preferred distinction was between propositions, which are either true or false, and statements, which need be neither,[2] and I will use

---

[1] On their difficulties, see Cohen (1976)   [2] Ayer (1946) pp. 5–9

the same distinction in what follows. If it were possible to show that there is after all no feasible distinction of the necessary kind, that would merely be an alternative argument for the conclusion about verificationism which I shall actually reach.

In general, the sceptic denies us the power to gain some type of cognitive *rapport* with propositions of a certain type – no contingent propositions are objects of knowledge, no propositions entailing the existence of material things are objects of justified belief, and so on. The verificationist thinks that our ability to gain some type of cognitive *rapport* either with a proposition or its negation is a necessary condition for that proposition to exist at all. And whenever sceptic and verificationist are talking of one and the same type of cognitive *rapport*, it is open to the verificationist to claim that the sceptic's position is either undisturbing or false. For surely, he may argue, there is nothing disturbing about not having a cognitive rapport with a proposition unless there is actually a possibly false proposition, which, not having this benefit, one is nevertheless liable to believe. We do not want knowledge, justified belief, assurance of truth or whatever for its own sake, but rather to avoid the disappointments which are liable to follow from believing what is false. And if not having the cognitive *rapport* means also that there is no false proposition to believe, it likewise eliminates the corresponding possibilities of an unpleasant surprise.

To apply this general argument to scepticism about radical assurance, the verificationist must hold that it is a necessary condition for a sentence to be meaningful that we can radically assure ourselves either that the statement it expresses is true, or radically assure ourselves that the statement it expresses is false. Then, faced with the thesis that there are hardly any propositions which we can β-assure ourselves and hence radically assure ourselves to be true, he replies that the things which it disturbingly looked as though we would have to believe without radical assurance are either not possibly false propositions at all, but mere statements which are neither true nor false, or genuine propositions after all, which despite appearances we can either β-assure ourselves to be true, or β-assure ourselves to be false.

As in any employment of the same general argument, the verificationist must assume that there is no intrinsic value in the cognitive rapport which the sceptic denies us. But whatever one thinks in general about the value of radical assurance, the verificationist argument does look distinctly unpromising in its present application. For one thing, our present, or as we can call him radical assurance verificationist seems obliged to deny the highly plausible principle that no proposition of the form '*p* is self-evident' is itself self-evident (see p. 46 above). This principle must be denied by any radical assurance verificationist who thinks that radical and β-assurance have a co-extensive scope. For it follows from this principle that

(A) No proposition of the form 'we can β-assure ourselves either that *p* or that not-*p*' is itself a proposition which we can β-assure ourselves to be true or β-assure ourselves to be false

And the radical assurance verificationist must I think either reject (A), or accept that his own doctrine is a mere statement which is neither true nor false, or accept that

(B) Radical assurance verificationism is a proposition which we can β-assure ourselves to be true or β-assure ourselves to be false

is a mere statement which is neither true nor false. For radical assurance verificationism entails (B) if they are both either true or false. And if both radical assurance verificationism and (B) are either true or false, it follows from the former that (B) is a proposition which we can β-assure ourselves to be true or β-assure ourselves to be false, which is incompatible with (A).

There is another implausibility, common both to radical assurance verificationism and verificationisms determined by a weaker concept of assurance. Let us define a *U*-proposition as a proposition which no one ever has or ever will assure himself to be true. The following sentence seems to express a proposition, as opposed to a mere statement: 'For every four true *U*-propositions, there are five false *U*-propositions'. But it looks as though this sentence expresses something which it is logically impossible for anyone to assure himself to be true. A necessary condition for you to assure yourself of its truth would be that you had assured yourself, of some propositions, firstly that they were *U*-propositions, and secondly that they were true. And by the definition of a *U*-proposition, these two conditions cannot both be satisfied. So the verificationist must show that this sentence expresses something whose negation you can assure yourself to be true. And it looks as if the same two conditions would have to be satisfied in order for you to assure yourself that its negation was true.

More generally, it may well be that a sentence expresses a proposition only if there is some proposition which is evidence for the truth or falsity of what that sentence expresses. It may even be that no one is entitled to believe that a sentence expresses a proposition unless he actually possesses a means for somehow settling the truth-value of what it expresses. But it does not follow from either of these doctrines that a sentence cannot express a proposition unless someone is able to settle the truth-value of what it expresses, or even that a man cannot believe a proposition and at the same time be entitled to believe that this proposition is not one whose truth-value we can somehow settle.

I can be slightly briefer with the neo-Kantian sector of the standard dialectic of self-defeat.

> The idea of a predicate is correlative with that of a *range* of distinguishable individuals of which the predicate can be significantly, though not necessarily truly, affirmed.[1]
>
> It is a quite general truth that the ascription of different states or determinations to an identical subject turns on the existence of some means of distinguishing or identifying the subject of such descriptions as one object among others.[2]
>
> There would be no question of ascribing one's own states of consciousness, or experiences, to anything, unless one also ascribed, or were ready and able to ascribe, states of consciousness, or experiences, to other individual entities of the same logical type as that thing to which one ascribes one's own states of consciousness. The condition of reckoning oneself as a subject of such predicates is that one should also reckon others as subjects of such predicates. The condition, in turn, of this being possible, is that one should be able to distinguish from one another, to pick out or identify, different subjects of such predicates, i.e. different individuals of the type concerned.[3]

To anyone hoping that scepticism about radical assurance may defeat itself, the second of these three passages will suggest the following principle:

[1] Strawson (1959) p. 99n
[2] Strawson (1966) p. 102
[3] Strawson (1959) p. 104

(B) If I can be β-assured that something is true of a particular concrete object, then I can be β-assured that other concrete objects exist as well

And the third passage will suggest

(C) If I can be β-assured that something is true of myself, then I can be β-assured that other people exist as well

Suppose we liberalise the initial assumptions about the scope of self-evidence to the extent of allowing that I can be β-assured that I am thinking. Then if either (B) or (C) is true it follows, unexpectedly, that I can be β-assured that other concrete objects exist besides me.

Strawson's second passage is part of a more ambitious flight of thought. 'It is a quite general truth that the ascription of different states or determinations to an identical subject turns on the existence of some means of distinguishing or identifying the subject of such descriptions as one object among others.' 'Experience of the object-ive' requires us to have 'empirically applicable criteria of persistence and identity', to 'have and apply concepts of substances'.[1] It is also true that if we can draw an 'effective distinction . . . between object-ive and subjective time-orders', there must be 'co-existence of objects of possible with objects of actual perception'.[2] Finally, we are to consider what follows if 'we add to the idea of unperceived objective co-existence . . . the idea of perceived objective succession or change'. It is that 'while . . . perceptions of the world may reveal *some* objective changes which we can characterise as inexplicable, they can do so only against a background of persistences and altera-tions which we recognise as explicable, predictable and regular'.[3] If this further reasoning is sound then the truth of (B) may allow me to conclude not merely that I can be β-assured that there exist concrete objects other than myself, but also that I am part of a lawfully changing plurality of objects. It begins to look as though, with only a slight liberalisation of my initial assumptions about the scope of self-evidence, we can enormously extend the scope of β-assurance, significantly narrow the gap between the radical assurance we are liable to want and the radical assurance we are able to get, and approach the point at which it is trivial and no longer disturbing to assert that radical and β-assurance have a co-extensive scope.

[1] Strawson (1966) p. 132
[2] ibid. p. 141
[3] Strawson (1966) pp. 143–4

The difficulty is simply to find grounds for accepting that either (B) or (C) is true. Numerous critics have pointed to the complete absence in Strawson's own works of any adequate argument for any of the various possible interpretations of the two passages, by which (B) and (C) were suggested.[1] And there are difficulties enough anyway in the further argument to a lawfully changing plurality.[2]

(2) *Ostensive definition*

Suppose we liberalise our initial assumptions about the scope of self-evidence to the extent of allowing that I can β-assure myself that I understand a sentence. The scope of β-assurance might then be expandable a good deal further. One can imagine an argument to the effect that, even on unrevised assumptions about the scope of self-evidence, I can β-assure myself that 'I understand a sentence' is evidence for a proposition entailing the existence of some concrete objects other than myself. And if I can β-assure myself of the truth of that proposition about evidence, and also β-assure myself that I understand a sentence, then I can β-assure myself that there is a concrete object other than myself. For if I can β-assure myself that q and that q is evidence for p, then perhaps I can also β-assure myself that p.

What is the argument for the proposition that 'I understand a sentence' is evidence for a proposition entailing the existence of some concrete object other than myself? Taking 'ϕ-proposition' to stand for any proposition entailing the existence of some concrete object other than myself, it runs as follows:

(1) 'I understand a sentence' is evidence for 'There is some sentence-type, capable of expressing ϕ-propositions, which was introduced into my language ostensively'

(2) I can β-assure myself that 'Sentences of a certain type were introduced into my language ostensively' is evidence of 'In the introductory situations someone used sentences of that type to assert ϕ-propositions, and most of these ϕ-propositions are true'

(3) I can β-assure myself that 'I understand a sentence' is evidence for 'Some ϕ-propositions or other are true' (from (1) and (2))

[1] See especially Plantinga (1967) pp. 205–11, 227–32   [2] See Mackie (1974) Ch. 4

(4) 'Some ϕ-propositions or other are true' is itself a ϕ-proposition

(5) I can β-assure myself that 'I understand a sentence' is evidence for a ϕ-proposition (from (3) and (4))

You may think it possible to go even further than this. Suppose that if sentences of type X were introduced into my language ostensively, then I have become disposed to respond to experiences like those I had in the introductory situations by using X-type sentences to assert ϕ-propositions. Given (2) it would then seem that usually, when experience prompts me to use such a sentence in order to assert a ϕ-proposition, that proposition will be true. Since I can β-assure myself that this last principle is true, and also β-assure myself that experience has just prompted me to use an ostensively-introduced sentence type to assert a ϕ-proposition, I can β-assure myself that that same ϕ-proposition is true.

Something rather like this fuller version of the argument is defended by Quinton in the treatment of language-acquisition which I referred to in the previous chapter (see pp. 97–8 above). One point of difference is that according to Quinton if sentences of a certain type were introduced into my language ostensively then in the introductory situations someone will have been 'justified by experience' in believing propositions expressed by sentences of that type, and whenever experiences occur which resemble these original justifying experiences and combine with my training to prompt the assertive use of sentences of that type, then these experiences will once more justify me in believing the propositions I assert. The propositions expressed by these sentence-types will according to Quinton entail the existence of concrete objects other than myself and they will have what he calls 'experiential probability', a probability which, though relational, is not 'a relation to a belief, to other statements', is not propositional in nature.[1] But the essential idea can I think be stated without using the notion of justification by experience, and its correlative notion of experiential probability. There seems no difference between being justified by experience in believing p and believing p in experiential circumstances such that the proposition that one believes p in these circumstances is evidence for p's truth (see pp. 97–8 above).

There is however no point in trying to go beyond (1)–(5) if not

[1] Quinton (1973) p. 160

even that much is secure. And in fact two of the premisses of (1)–(5) are very doubtful indeed. Why, to begin with, should we accept

> (2) I can β-assure myself that 'Sentences of a certain type were introduced into my language ostensively' is evidence for 'In the introductory situations someone used sentences of that type to assert ϕ-propositions, and most of these ϕ-propositions are true'?

Perhaps it would be gratuitously complex to suppose that an apparatus of deception operates in the introductory situations and ensures that the ϕ-propositions asserted in these situations are for the most part false. But there is a difference between not saying that most members of a set of propositions are false, and saying that most members of a set of propositions are true. And why in any case should you be able to β-assure yourself that the simplicity of a hypothesis is evidence for its truth?

The other doubtful premiss is

> (1) 'I understand a sentence' is evidence for 'there is some sentence-type, capable of expressing ϕ-propositions, which was introduced into my language ostensively'

Quinton himself thinks that the necessity of ostensively introduced sentence-types is established by an analogue of 'the old difficulty about the regress of justification'.[1] But he is not very explicit about what the old difficulty is actually supposed to be. If the non-ostensive introduction of a sentence-type into one's language involves one in a task which takes an infinite time to complete, then one would need to have performed an infinite number of these tasks if no sentence-type is ostensively introduced. But as I pointed out when I was discussing the impossibility of α-assurance, my initial assumptions about self-evidence do not allow us to β-assure ourselves that a man cannot perform an infinite number of tasks in a finite time (see p. 58 above).

(3) *Private languages*

Consider the following conditional: 'If I can be β-assured that I have just used some sentence correctly, then some concrete object other than myself exists'. On the initial assumptions about self-

[1] ibid pp. 216, 126

evidence, I cannot be β-assured that the antecedent of this conditional is true, because no proposition of the form '*p* is self-evident' is itself self-evident, and so I cannot be β-assured of the truth of any proposition of the form 'I can be β-assured that *p*'. But suppose we liberalise the initial assumptions about self-evidence at this point, and allow that I can be β-assured that the antecedent of the conditional is true. If the whole conditional is necessarily true, and if I can be β-assured that its antecedent is true, then perhaps I can also be β-assured of its consequent, which would once more give us an unexpected and promising expansion in the scope of β-assurance. Let us at any rate see what can be said for the necessity of the conditional.

Wittgenstein seems to have held that I cannot know or be justified in believing that I have just used a word correctly to stand for a sensation, unless at least some part of my language is public. It must be public in the sense that the meanings of the words it contains are so related to my behaviour that if someone other than me existed, he could understand these meanings by observing my behaviour. It might seem as though I could confirm that I have just used a word correctly in naming or describing a particular sensation by appealing to my memory that I originally associated that word with sensations like the particular sensation I have named or described, and that this procedure would be possible whether or not there was the relation in question between the meaning of my sensation words and my external behaviour. But, according to Wittgenstein, this would not be genuine confirmation. It would be 'as if someone were to buy several copies of the morning paper to assure himself that what it said was true'.[1] If Wittgenstein's thesis about confirmation is correct, it seems to follow that it is a necessary condition for me to know or justifiably believe that sensation-words have a meaning that some concrete object other than myself exists. There has to be behaviour on my part through which anyone who was there to observe it could understand the meanings of my sensation words, and this behaviour will presumably be interaction with a physical environment which exists independently of me. There is a chance, then, that we may be able to convert Wittgenstein's argument for his thesis about confirmation into an argument for the necessity of the conditional I began with.

Wittgenstein seems also to have held that it is a necessary

---

[1] Wittgenstein (1958) section 265

condition for it to be meaningful to say that I have just used a sensation word correctly that I can know or be justified in believing that I have. But we do not need to consider the defensibility of the full and apparently verificationist anti-private language doctrine. It is enough for present purposes if we can extract grounds for the necessity of my initial conditional from that part of the doctrine which is concerned with the conditions for knowing, by adducing evidence, that one's usage of sensation words is correct. I will call this part of Wittgenstein's doctrine 'the evidence thesis'.

The actual text of the *Philosophical Investigations* suggests two separate arguments for the evidence thesis. The first, which I will call the infallibility argument, is suggested by section 258.

> Let us imagine the following case. I want to keep a diary about the recurrence of a certain sensation. To this end I associate it with the sign '*S*' and write this sign in a calendar for every day on which I have the sensation. I will remark first of all that a definition of the sign cannot be formulated. But still I can give myself a kind of ostensive definition. How? Can I point to the sensation? Not in the ordinary sense. But I speak, or write the sign down, and at the same time I concentrate my attention on the sensation – and so, as it were, point to it inwardly. But what is this ceremony for? For that is all it seems to be! A definition surely serves to establish the meaning of a sign. Well, that is done precisely by the concentrating of my attention; for in this way I impress on myself the connexion between the sign and the sensation. But 'I impress it on myself' can only mean: this process brings it about that I remember the connexion right in the future. But in the present case I have no criterion of correctness. One would like to say: whatever is going to seem right to me is right. And that only means that here we can't talk about 'right'.

We suppose that my language is private and that I have given the word '*S*' a meaning by associating it with certain sensations, by 'impressing on myself' the connexion between the sign and the sensation. The associative process 'brings it about that I remember the connexion right in the future'. That is to say, the process gives me the habit of not actually calling a sensation an '*S*' unless it is precisely a sensation of the type which figures in that process. Later on, after the associative process is completed, I have a sensation and call it an '*S*'. It seems to me that I have used the word '*S*' correctly on this particular occasion but I wonder whether I really have. But if my language is private and if I do in general understand the meaning of '*S*', then an associative process has occurred which *guarantees* that whenever I have a sensation and call it an '*S*', then I use '*S*' correctly. So, if *these* are the circumstances in which '*S*' seemed the right word, '*S*' *was* the right word. In circumstances like *these*, 'whatever is going to seem right to me is right'. But in this case I cannot confirm or cite *evidence* for the proposition that on this particular occasion I used '*S*' correctly. For citing evidence is something you do after or in the course of an investigation, and there is no point in carrying out an investigation into the truth value of a proposition if the mere fact that it has *seemed* true at some stage prior to the investigation is enough to guarantee its truth.

This interpretation of Section 258 does, I think, also fit the notorious Section 265.

> Let us imagine a table (something like a dictionary) that exists only in our imagination. A dictionary can be used to justify the translation of a word *X* by a word *Y*. But are we also to call it a justification if such a table is to be looked up only in the imagination? – 'Well, yes; then it is a subjective justification.' – But justification consists in appealing to something independent. – 'But surely I can appeal from one memory to another. For example, I don't know if I have remembered the time of departure of a train right and to check it I call to mind how a page of the time-table looked. Isn't it the same here?' No; for this process has got to produce a memory which is actually correct. If the mental image of the time-table could not itself be tested for correctness, how could it confirm the correctness of the first memory? (As if someone were to buy several copies of the morning paper to assure himself that what it said was true.)
>
> Looking up a table in the imagination is no more looking up a table, than the image of the result of an imagined experiment is the result of an experiment.

Once more we have a private language speaker who has given the word '*S*' a meaning by an associative process and therefore has a general understanding of what '*S*' means. Then on some subsequent occasion he calls a sensation an *S* and wonders whether in so doing he has used '*S*' correctly. Searching for evidence, he casts his mind back to see if he can remember the original associative process. But the effort of memory is completely futile because if it succeeds, and he does remember the original associative process, then he remembers something whose occurrence is already guaranteed by the fact that he is a private language speaker with a general understanding of '*S*' who has just been prompted to call a sensation an *S*. Furthermore, his calling the sensation he has just had an *S* involved his believing or imagining that it was the sort of sensation he originally associated with '*S*'. And this believing or imagining will continue to accompany the conscious effort to remember that he now makes. But we have already seen that, in the circumstances, this believing or imagining cannot but be a believing or imagining of the truth, i.e. itself a remembering of the associative process. So the additional conscious effort to remember the process is redundant. And this is what makes it like buying several copies of the morning paper in order to assure oneself that what it says is true. What is the difference between the man who wonders whether he has remembered the train time correctly and tries to check up by visualising a page of the timetable and the private language speaker who wonders whether he has just used '*S*' correctly and tries to check up by consulting his imaginary quasi-dictionary, casting his mind back to the original associative effort? The difference is that the first man can visualise the page wrongly, whereas the private language speaker, given that he has a general understanding of '*S*', and has called a sensation an *S*, will always succeed in remembering the sort of sensation in question when he consults his quasi-dictionary. And the factors which guarantee that he does remember also prevent the proposition that he does remember from functioning as evidence.

But section 265 also suggests a second argument for the evidence thesis, which I will call the fallibility argument. If we interpret section 265 in this second way, then the difficulty about consulting the quasi-dictionary is not so much that there is no proposition which it enables the private language speaker to cite as evidence, but rather that he needs, but cannot get, some further evidence for the evidence it enables him to cite. His attempted visualising of the train timetable yields, as evidence, a proposition to the effect that he remembers seeing a certain time on the page, and he can provide further evidence for this last proposition by looking up the actual physical page. But in the quasi-dictionary case he cannot provide any *further* evidence for the proposition that the sensation he has just called an *S* was of the sort he originally associated with '*S*'. He must simply make the fallible claim that this is what he remembers. On the fallibility interpretation 'has got to' in 'this process has got to produce a memory which is *correct*' means 'ought to': if the attempt to visualise a train timetable or to consult a quasi-dictionary is to yield good evidence, it must produce a genuine and veridical memory; and in the quasi-dictionary case we are fatally unable to know, by adducing further evidence, that this condition is satisfied. On the infallibility interpretation, 'has got to' means 'inevitably will': the private language speaker's process of consulting the quasi-dictionary is simply the redundant reinforcing of a memory which is already inevitably correct, and whose inevitable correctness makes it pointless for him to adduce any evidence for the correctness of his usage. In 'this process has got to produce a memory which is *correct*', 'this process' refers to the private language speaker's effort to check up by casting his mind back, not to a type of process of which both that effort and the attempted visualisation of the train timetable are instances.

Neither argument seems cogent. The fallibility argument, as has often been pointed out, tells equally against the possibility of knowing that one has used a word of a public language correctly. For here too one would need to rely in the end either on claims to remember or at any rate on some fallible evidence for which no further evidence can be provided.[1] The infallibility argument appeals to the principle that you cannot properly be said to cite evidence for p if, prior to any investigation of p's truth-value, the fact that p has seemed to you true guarantees that p is true. But there is no reason in general why your investigation of p's truth-value should not consist precisely in an investigation of the relation between p's truth-value and the fact that p seems to you true. If, as a private language speaker, I want sufficient evidence for

(1) In describing the sensation I have just had as an S I used the word 'S' correctly

there is indeed no reason why I should not cite the conjunctive proposition '"S" seemed the right word, and I do in general understand the meaning of the word "S" and my language is private'. I may, of course, want further evidence for this conjunctive proposition, and it is difficult to imagine what this further evidence would be. But the infallibility argument is not that I want but cannot get

[1] See Ayer (1963) pp. 41–2; cf. Fogelin (1976) p. 162

further evidence for the evidence I cite, but rather that there is no proposition which I can properly be said to cite as <u>evidence in the</u> first place.

Is there in fact a proposition which, as a private language speaker, I can cite as evidence for (1), and for which I will not want further evidence? The natural candidate is the one which the fallibility argument tries unsuccessfully to exclude, namely that I remember that

> (2) The sensation I have just had and described as an *S* was of the type I originally associated with the word '*S*'

And if, as a private language speaker, I want further evidence for

> (3) I remember that (2)

then it is not clear how even as a public language speaker, I would have been able to terminate a regress of assurance for the proposition that I have just used a word of my language correctly.

But now a further argument suggests itself. Surely, if my language is private, then (2) and

> (1) In describing the sensation I have just had as an *S* I used the word '*S*' correctly

taken as sentences, will express one and the same proposition. And in this case

> (3) I remember that (2)

cannot be evidence for the proposition expressed by (1), because the argument from (3) to that proposition is normally question-begging. Any normally intelligent man who was doubtful about the truth of *p* would thereby be made equally doubtful about the truth of '*N* remembers that *p*' (see p. 27 above). (Kenny, in his explanation of section 265, seems at one point to attribute this further argument to Wittgenstein himself:

> We are supposing that I wish to justify my calling a private sensation '*S*' by appealing to a mental table in which memory-samples or private objects of various kinds are listed in correlation with symbols . . . To make use of such a table one must call up the right memory-sample: e.g. I must make sure to call up the memory-sample that belongs alongside '*S*' and not the one which belongs to '*T*'. But as this table exists only in the imagination,

there can be no real looking up to see which sample goes with '*S*'. All there can be is remembering which sample goes with '*S*', i.e. *remembering what 'S' means*. But this is precisely what the table was supposed to confirm. In other words, the memory of the meaning of '*S*' is being used to confirm itself.[1])

Or, in a slightly more plausible development of the same idea, one and the same proposition is expressed by

(1) In describing the sentence I have just had as an *S* I used the word '*S*' correctly

and

(4) Either (2) the sensation I have just had and described as an *S* was of the type I originally associated with the word '*S*', or the sensation I have just had and described as an *S* was of the type which is called an *S* as a matter of public convention

Once again,

(3) I remember that (2)

cannot be evidence for the proposition expressed by (1), because the argument '"*N* remembers that *p*" therefore "*p* or *q*"' is just as question-begging as the argument '"*N* remembers that *p*" therefore *p*'.

What, however, is the criterion of propositional identity, on which one and the same proposition is expressed by (1) and (4)? The two sentences might express the same proposition if logical equivalence is a sufficient condition for propositional identity. But that has the paradoxical consequence that all necessarily true propositions are identical. Should we perhaps say that two sentences express the same proposition only if it is true both that the proposition expressed by each strictly implies the proposition expressed by the other, and that every semantically simple element in the one sentence should be either synonymous with some set of semantically simple elements in the other or part of a set of semantically simple elements with which some semantically simple element in the other is synonymous? Or that the proposition expressed by each must strictly imply the proposition expressed by the other, and necessarily anyone who believes the proposition expressed by one believes

[1] Kenny (1973) pp. 192–3

the proposition expressed by the other?[1] Neither of these tests is passed by (1) and (4).

I think it is reasonable to conclude that either the public language speaker cannot get satisfactory evidential assurance that he is using the words of his language correctly or the private language speaker can get satisfactory evidential assurance that in describing the sensation he has just had as an S he has used the word 'S' correctly, by citing as evidence that he remembers that the sensation he has just had and described as an S was of the type he originally associated with the word S. If this is right then Wittgenstein's anti-private language doctrine does not establish the necessary truth of the conditional 'If I can be β-assured that I have just used some sentence correctly, then some concrete object other than myself exists', and hence cannot be adapted to extend the scope of β-assurance. And this, I think, exhausts the resources of the standard dialectic of self-defeat.

[1] cf. Blackburn (1975) pp. 197–205

6

Induction

Traditional scepticisms fail to engage with the more stable cognitive desires we are liable to have, and depend on the limited applicability of concepts of knowledge, justification or rationality which no one other than the sceptic himself would want, or more than briefly want, to make an extensive use of. That was my initial claim, and my effort so far has been to articulate and defend a less arbitrary kind of sceptical doctrine. But possibly the whole contrast is overdone. There is the sceptic who thinks that foundations of knowledge or justified belief are both necessary and impossible, and there is the sceptic who doubts the rationality of some or all of the inferences by means of which the rest of our belief-system would in any case have to be generated. If scepticism about radical assurance is, with qualifications, foundational, are there not also non-arbitrary and indeed highly traditional scepticisms of a purely inferential kind? The present chapter attempts to answer this question, so far as it concerns the inductive inference of theoretical propositions. Its application to moral propositions will be discussed in Chapter 7.

Inductive scepticism, in a vague but typical formulation, is the doctrine that we cannot be inferentially justified in believing any proposition by virtue of having inductive evidence for its truth. And in the interests of generality we might as well take 'q is inductive evidence for p' to mean simply 'q is evidence for p but does not entail p'. This usage excludes the customary juxtaposition of inductive and 'criterial' evidence, but, as we will see later on (see pp. 144, 150–1 below), there is no reason to think that this is a very substantial disadvantage. Inductive sceptics differ, of course, on the necessary conditions of inferential justification in general. But they would perhaps agree that N is inferentially justified in believing p only if there is another proposition q which satisfies the condition

(A) N believes q

together with one or both of the conditions

(B) q is overriding evidence for p

and

(C) N believes that q is overriding evidence for p

where q is overriding evidence for p if it is stronger evidence for p than any true proposition is for *not-p* (see p. 29 above). And we can say that N is inferentially justified in believing p by virtue of having inductive evidence, or for short inductively justified in believing p, if he is inferentially justified in believing p and the only proposition q which satisfies both (A) and whichever of (B) and (C) it has to satisfy is a proposition which either is, or is believed by N to be, overriding inductive evidence for p. The essential claim of inductive scepticism will then be that if N is inductively justified in believing p then at least one of two further conditions must be satisfied but is either completely unsatisfiable or cannot be very often satisfied. The two further conditions are

(D) N is justified in believing q

and

(E) N is justified in believing that q is overriding inductive evidence for p

The most obvious method of inductive scepticism is in a broad sense Humean. You assume that condition (E) must be satisfied if N is to be inductively justified in believing p, and then argue that (E) cannot be satisfied because (i) no one can be justified in believing a contingent proposition of the form

(1) q is inductive evidence for p

and (ii) no form (1) proposition is necessarily true.

A second and non-Humean method of inductive scepticism is to assume that if N is inductively justified in believing p, then it is true that both

(D) N is justified in believing q

and

(E) N is justified in believing that q is overriding inductive evidence for p

and then claim that although both (D) and (E) may be satisfiable

separately, it is highly unlikely if not impossible that they will both
be satisfied at the same time. One argument would be that (E) is
satisfiable only if there is a true proposition of the form

(1) *q* is inductive evidence for *p*

but that whenever we have a true proposition of form (1), then
either the proposition *q* which it refers to is likely to be false, which
would prevent (D) from being satisfied, or, if the proposition *q*
which it refers to is true, then there is a true proposition q_1, such
that q_1 is as strong inductive evidence for *not-p* as *q* is for *p*, which
will make it false that *q* is overriding inductive evidence for *p* (see
p. 29 above), and hence prevent (E) from being satisfied.

The question I want to discuss in this chapter is whether either of
these two methods of inductive scepticism is both feasible and
independent of my scepticism about radical assurance. Someone
says that, thanks to an argument of one or other of these two kinds,
he is justified in believing that inductive scepticism is true. Which,
if any, of my theses about radical assurance does this commit him to
accepting?

My chief aim in posing this question is to provide a context or
location for scepticism about radical assurance. But of course the
question would have additional interest if you were seriously uncertain about the actual truth of scepticism about radical assurance.
If you did finally accept my doubts about radical assurance, then the
soundness of inductive scepticism will hardly be an additional
sorrow. It is true that even my initial assumptions about the scope
of self-evidence do not exclude the possibility that some form (1)
propositions are ones that we can β-assure ourselves to be true (see
p.45 above). And the inductive sceptic may now have his own
autonomous arguments to rule this out. But there is not much value
in being able to β-assure yourself that a form (1) proposition is true
when there is so little else for which you can have the sort of
assurance you are liable to want. If on the other hand you were
uncertain about the truth-value of my theses on radical assurance,
you now face the question of whether a more restricted and purely
inductive scepticism can be established by arguments of a less
doubtful quality. And one way of reassuring yourself that it cannot
be would be to show that the only good arguments for inductive
scepticism are ones which would commit you to the very theses on
radical assurance whose truth-value you were unable to decide.

In section (1) I suggest that it is difficult to carry out the first stage of the Humean method without accepting that extensive radical assurance is something we are liable to want. But this suggestion of heteronomy is inconclusive, and so in section (2) I ask whether the Humean method does not in any case break down in its second stage. Section (3) is about the autonomy and feasibility of the other, non-Humean, method of inductive scepticism.

The Humean's claim that there are no necessarily true propositions of the form

(1) q is inductive evidence for p

is not of course supposed to be a mere consequence of the fact that it is never necessarily true that one proposition is any kind of evidence for another. And yet it probably is the case that all true propositions of the form 'q is evidence for p' are contingent, if 'evidence' is being used in either the ordinary or the liberalised senses which I described in Chapter 1. For I said there that q is evidence for p only if (iv) the argument 'q therefore p' is not normally question-begging, i.e. only if a normally intelligent man with antecedent doubts about p's truth would not thereby be made equally doubtful about the truth of q. But it is not clear that this condition (iv) can be satisfied anything but contingently unless we actually define 'normally intelligent' so that you are not normally intelligent if your antecedent doubts about p's truth are alleviated by any of the sorts of arguments which (iv) might otherwise have been expected contingently to exclude, e.g. arguments to a disjunctive p from one of its disjuncts, arguments of the form '(q and r) therefore p' or '(*not-r* or p) and r, therefore p'. I propose then, for the rest of this and the next chapter, to use 'evidence' in a sense which is exactly like the liberalised sense I defined in Chapter 1 except that it is not determined by condition (iv). The achievement of evidential assurance will still require the use of arguments which are not normally question-begging, and the Humean will be able to exploit this fact. But he will not have to state his arguments about induction and necessity in the cumbersome form of arguments for the conclusion that, of those necessary conditions for the truth of a proposition of the form 'q is evidence for p' which are either necessarily satisfied or necessarily not satisfied, none is necessarily satisfied when the evidence in question is inductive.

(1) *The autonomy of Humean scepticism*

The Humean method of inductive scepticism is to assume that N is inductively justified in believing p only if he is also justified in believing that q is overriding inductive evidence for p, and then argue that (i) no one can be justified in believing a contingent proposition of the form

(1) q is inductive evidence for p

and (ii) no form (1) proposition is necessarily true. The putative obstacle to justified belief in a form (1) contingency is either question-beggingness or vicious infinite regression.

But what, in this context, *is* justified belief? And why should the contingency of a form (1) proposition make its justified acceptance so problematical? One way of answering these questions would be this. 'Justified belief' means 'radical assurance of truth'; we are liable to want radical assurance of the truth of a form (1) proposition when we have evidential assurance of an inductive kind because we are liable, when considering the character of our belief-system as a whole, to want radical assurance of the truth of the essential core of our belief-system (see pp. 66–71 above); the contingency of form (1) propositions makes it impossible to have radical assurance of their truth because all radical assurance is of either the α- or the β-kind, regressive considerations eliminate α-assurance, and there are hardly any contingent propositions of whose truth we can gain β-assurance. Must the Humean inductive sceptic answer like this, and thus lose his autonomy, or can he find some cogent answer of an entirely different kind?

One possibility would be for him to take justified belief as a kind of passive analogue of assurance. You are justified in believing p only if p is true and you are caused to believe p either by what makes it true or by the believing of some true proposition which is evidence for p and which you are justified in believing. We then have an analogue of the distinction between α- and β-assurance. You are α-justified in believing p if and only if you are justified in believing p but not β-justified in believing p. You are β-justified in believing p if and only if either (i) you are caused to believe p by what makes it true, or (ii) there is a proposition which you are caused to believe by what makes it true, your believing of which causes you to believe p, and which is evidence either for p, or for a proposition which is

evidence for p, or . . . We are liable to want justified belief in a form
(1) proposition whenever we have inferential justification of an
inductive kind because we are liable to want all our beliefs to be non-
coincidentally true. It is not possible to be justified in believing a
contingent form (1) proposition, because α-justification is impossible, and there are no form (1) propositions among the contingencies which we can be β-justified in believing.

But I doubt whether this is really a firm support for inductive
scepticism. Firstly, I deny that, in wanting non-coincidentally true
belief, we want simply to be caused to believe what is true, rather
than actively to assure ourselves of the truth (see p. 67 above).
And secondly, it is not clear how we would actually prove that α-
justification is impossible. Why is it impossible for a man to be
caused to believe p by his believing of q, caused to believe q by his
believing of q_1, and so on *ad infinitum*, each proposition in the series
being both true and evidence for its predecessor if it has one? If 'N
is justified in believing p' is defined in a way which does not require
N either to do anything or to be able to do anything, then there
seems no cogent objection to an infinite regress of justification (see
p. 67 above).

Alternatively, the Humean might interpret being justified in
believing a proposition as having assured yourself of its truth, and
then insist that whether or not you are more generally liable to want
your assurance to be radical, you cannot even gain a minimally
satisfactory non-radical assurance that a contingent proposition of
the form

(1) q is inductive evidence for p

is true.

There are two ways in which he might try to make good this
claim. One would be to try to show that you would be crippled by
vicious infinite regression, the other that you would have to depend
on a question-begging argument.

The first premiss in the sceptic's infinite regression line of thought
is that if a form (1) proposition is contingent, then you cannot
assure yourself of its truth in anything but an evidential way. A
purely sensory assurance is obviously impossible, and the only
contingent propositions of whose truth we can intuitively assure
ourselves are a few Cartesian vacuities like 'I exist'. Suppose then
that our assurance of truth for a form (1) contingency must be

evidential. We will also want to be assured of the truth of the proposition we cite as evidence for the form (1) contingency. A regress of assurance now threatens, and this regress is interminable, whether or not radical assurance is something we are more generally liable to want. Even if we would in general be as happy for the regress to terminate in sensory assurance, as in assurance of the intuitive kind, no terminating assurance of either kind is available in the present case. There is no proposition of whose truth we can have either sensory or intuitive assurance, which is also evidence for a form (1) contingency, or evidence for what is evidence for a form (1) contingency, or . . .

If the Humean argues in this way he does not, on the face of it, commit himself to the thesis that radical assurance is something we are liable to want. But I am still not sure that his argument is fully independent of that thesis. The difficulty is that he assumes, in at least two different stages of his argument, the regressive principle that you are evidentially assured of a proposition's truth only if you are assured of the truth of another proposition which you believe to be evidence for it. This principle is assumed early on in his argument, when he says that we will want to be assured of the truth of the proposition we cite in evidence for a form (1) contingency. And it also underlies the last part of his argument, where he talks as if the regress of assurance for a form (1) contingency would have to terminate in sensory or intuitive assurance even if the assurance in question is not radical. Someone who rejected the principle that you are evidentially assured that p only if you are assured of the truth of the proposition q which you believe to be evidence for p would want to know why a regress of assurance for a form (1) contingency cannot terminate in unassured affirmation. The Humean's tacit assumption of this principle casts doubt on the independence of his argument because it is not clear how he can actually show that we want, or are liable to want, an evidential assurance which conforms to it, without showing much more besides. We are liable to want radical assurance, and radical assurance conforms to his regressive principle. But what grounds are there for supposing that we want, or are liable to want, an assurance which conforms to his regressive principle, other than the grounds for supposing that we are liable to want radical assurance?

The Humean's other argument for the conclusion that we cannot gain a minimally satisfactory non-radical assurance for a form (1)

contingency is that any such assurance would have to be evidential
and that evidential assurance is excluded by the question-begging
character of any possible argument for a form (1) contingency.
More specifically, if you cite r as evidence for a contingent proposition of the form

(1) q is inductive evidence for p

you will also want to be assured that

(2) r is evidence for 'q is inductive evidence for p'

and you cannot be assured that (2) because all arguments of the form
'r therefore it is contingently true that q is inductive evidence for p'
are either normally question-begging, or at any rate likely to be
question-begging as addressed to you. That 'All past observed lions
are brown' is inductive evidence for 'the next lion to be observed will
be brown' is a contingent proposition of form (1). But you are not
going to be made any the less doubtful about it if someone cites as
evidence for it that all propositions of the form 'All past observed
As are Bs' are inductive evidence for propositions of the form 'The
next A to be observed will be a B'. And there is a similar defect in
any attempt to argue for a form (1) contingency.

This argument would of course be rejected by advocates of the
'inductive justification' of induction. But their most threatening-
looking counter-example seems defective. This depends on a distinction between different levels of argument. Arguments on level 1
are about individual things or events; for instance

(X_1) (q_1) All past observed lions have been brown
        (p_1) The next lion to be observed will be brown

Arguments on level 2 are about arguments on level 1; for instance

(X_2) (q_2) Arguments like X_1 which have been used to make pre-
               dictions in the past have given true conclusions from
               true premises most of the time
        (p_2) Arguments like X_1 will continue to give true conclu-
               sions from true premises most of the time

Arguments on level 3 are about arguments on level 2, and so on.
Now, suppose you have assured yourself that q_1. Then if you can
assure yourself that p_2, you can also assure yourself that q_1 is inductive evidence for p_1. But you can assure yourself that p_2 without

having already assured yourself that p_1 because you can assure yourself that q_2 and assure yourself of the truth of the conclusion of an appropriate inductive argument on level 3. In the same way, you can assure yourself of the truth of the conclusion of a level 3 argument without already having assured yourself that p_2. It is necessary only that you have assured yourself of the truth of the premiss of this level 3 argument and of the conclusion of the appropriate level 4 argument. And so on.[1] Given that you can assure yourself of the truth of the infinite set of propositions about the past q_1, q_2, q_3, . . . you can have evidential assurance of the truth of the form (1) proposition 'q_1 is inductive evidence for p_1' without begging the question.

But the objection is fallacious. The difficulty lies in the supposition that you can unproblematically assure yourself of the truth of (q_1 and q_2 and q_3 and . . .). The Humean might have been prepared to accept that you could assure yourself of the truth of this set of propositions if each of its members had really been about the past. But when the time references are made explicit, it turns out that q_3 is not really about the past at all. Suppose that you are evidentially assured at time t_1 that p_1, and q_2 is part of your evidence. Then what X_2 will actually have to mean is something like this:

$(X_2)^*$ (q_2) Up to t_1, arguments with premisses of the form 'All past observed As have been B' and with conclusions of the form 'The next A to be observed will be B' have given true conclusions from true premisses most of the time

   (p_2) After t_1, arguments with premisses of the form 'All past observed As have been B' and with conclusions of the form 'The next A to be observed will be B' will continue to give true conclusions from true premisses most of the time

And certainly, it is not a necessary condition for you to have assured yourself at t_1 that q_2 that you have already assured yourself that p_1. But can you really assure yourself at t_1 of the truth of the premiss of the level 3 argument without already having assured yourself that p_1? True enough, q_2 is about the time before t_1. But is the premiss of the appropriate level 3 argument about the time before t_1? This argument (X_3) will be

[1] Cf. Skyrms (1975), pp. 30–41

(q_3) Up to t_1 arguments like $(X_2)^*$ have given true conclusions from true premisses most of the time

(p_3) After t_1 arguments like $(X_2)^*$ will continue to give
true conclusions from true premisses most of the time

The trouble is that the conclusions of arguments like $(X_2)^*$ are
about the time after t_1, and so you cannot assure yourself that up to
t_1 they have given true conclusions from true premisses most of the
time unless you have already assured yourself of the truth of some
proposition about the time after t_1.

But even if it is true that all arguments of the form 'r therefore it is
contingently true that q is inductive evidence for p' are normally
question-begging, it is still doubtful whether, in appealing to this
fact, the Humean has emancipated himself from scepticism about
radical assurance. He takes it for granted that N cannot be inductively assured that p unless there is a proposition q such that N is
assured that q is inductive evidence for p. And this much we can
perhaps allow him without urging him to acknowledge the more
general regressive principle that you are evidentially assured of a
proposition's truth only if you are assured that another proposition
is evidence for it. But later on, when he tries by considerations about
question-beggingness to eliminate the possibility of evidential
assurance for a contingent proposition of the form

(1) q is inductive evidence for p

he assumes that you could not gain this evidential assurance unless
you were assured *that* some proposition r was evidence for the form
(1) contingency. By this stage he does seem to be assuming the more
general regressive principle I have just stated. We asked the
Humean who relied on considerations of vicious infinite regression
why we are supposed to want or be liable to want an evidential
assurance which conforms to the principle that you are evidentially
assured of a proposition's truth only if you are assured of the truth of
another proposition which you believe to be evidence for it. We
now ask the Humean who relies on considerations about question-
beggingness why we are supposed to want or be liable to want an
evidential assurance which conforms to the principle that you are
evidentially assured of a proposition's truth only if you are assured
that another proposition is evidence for it. In neither case is it clear
that he can answer our question without showing much more

besides. We are liable to want radical assurance of the truth of the essential core of our belief-systems, and radical assurance conforms to both of these regressive principles. But what grounds are there for supposing that we want or are liable to want an assurance which conforms to either regressive principle, other than the grounds for supposing that we are liable to want radical assurance?

You may think that although Humean inductive scepticism, as I have described it, is indeed doubtfully autonomous, this is only because I have in fact failed to mention one characteristically Humean argument altogether. This is that once someone does want assurance of the truth of a contingent proposition of the form

(1) q is inductive evidence for p

he would be irrational not to want it also for the proposition that r is evidence that q is inductive evidence for p, and want it on the same grounds, i.e. want it not because he accepts the general regressive principle that you are evidentially assured of a proposition's truth only if you are assured that another proposition is evidence for it, but simply because it is the inductiveness of the evidential relation which makes you want assurance that the form (1) contingency is true, and r will be inductive evidence for the form (1) contingency if evidence at all. I think this probably is a characteristically Humean point, but equally, I do not think that it provides very strong support for the thesis that there is no form (1) contingency that we can be justified in believing. For the mere fact that q does not entail p does not seem to provide any positive reason for wanting to be assured that it is evidence for p. Either you want to be assured that q is evidence for p simply because it is by adducing q as evidence that you are evidentially assured that p – a reason which would apply even if you thought that q might be deductive evidence, and which may or may not lead you also to want to be assured that r is evidence that q is evidence that p. Or you are happy to adduce q as evidence for p, even when it is merely inductive evidence, without wanting to be assured that it is evidence.

(2) *The feasibility of Humean scepticism*

The second stage of the Humean method is to argue that there are no necessarily true propositions of the form

(1) q is inductive evidence for p

You may think that there is no point in my considering arguments
against the existence of form (1) necessities until I have disposed of
the various grounds which philosophers have adduced for supposing
that they do exist. But there is in fact very little on that side actually
to criticise. There are misapplications of the 'meaning = use' thesis,
which have been thoroughly exposed by other writers.[1] And there
are claims about the existence of 'criterial evidence'. Although it is
customary to oppose criterial to inductive evidence, at least some
believers in criterial evidence would I think agree that q is criterial
evidence for p if (i) it is necessarily true that q is in my liberalised
sense inductive evidence for p; and (ii) if (i) were false it would be
impossible to have learnt the meaning of the type of sentence by
which p is expressed.[2] Others would insist that although (ii) is a
necessary condition, and although q cannot be criterial evidence for
p when it entails p, (i) and (ii) are not jointly sufficient because it is
also necessary that criterial evidence is conclusive evidence: 'if q
C-supports p and somebody knows that q is true, then he is fully
justified in claiming to know that p is true'.[3] But let us look more
closely at condition (ii). Suppose we grant that you could not have
learned the meaning of 'This is blue', unless there is a proposition
which describes the experience you had and which is in my liberalised sense inductive evidence for a proposition entailing the existence of a blue object. Why should it follow that it is necessarily true
that the experiential proposition is this sort of evidence? Why can
you not learn the meaning of 'this is blue' by having experiences as
of bilberries, cloudless skies, etc., even though it is no part of the
meaning of 'this is blue' that usually at least a proposition of the
kind it expresses is true when some such experiential proposition is
true? Not knowing of any answers to these questions, I move on
directly to what the Humean can say against the existence of
necessarily true propositions of form (1).

(a) *Moore's method*

The only possible ground I can think of for supposing that there
are no necessarily true propositions of the form

(1) q is inductive evidence for p

is the universal efficacy of a method analogous to that by which

---

[1] See especially Blackburn (1973) Ch. 1   [2] See Kenny (1967)
[3] Baker (1974) p. 163 (q and p transposed).

Moore thought we could show the non-identity of Good to any natural or metaphysical property. I am here following out a suggestion of Blackburn's, who appeals to a similar analogy in his attack on the rather different thesis that normative propositions to the effect it is right to have more confidence in p on believing q are analysable in terms of propositions to the effect that q is actually used as a reason for believing p.[1]

In *Principia Ethica* Moore claimed in effect to have found a method which would show, for every natural or metaphysical property F, the falsity of the corresponding proposition 'To be good is to be F'. As he subsequently explained, a natural property 'is a property with which it is the business of the natural sciences or of psychology to deal, or which can be completely defined in terms of such ... [and] a metaphysical property is a property which stands to some super-sensible object in the same relations in which natural properties stand to natural objects'.[2] On one interpretation, Moore's method would be to answer the thesis that to be good is to be F with the argument that if this were true then, absurdly, the proposition

(a) To be good is to be one of the things which are F

would be identical to the proposition

(b) To be one of the things which are F is to be one of things which are F

On another interpretation, his method would be to argue that if to be good is to be F, then, absurdly, the proposition

(c) A thing is good if and only if it is one of the things which are F

would be identical to the proposition

(d) A thing is one of the things which are F if and only if it is one of the things which are F

The main difference between the two methods is that the sentences used to express (c) and (d) are extensional, while the sentences used to express (a) and (b) are not extensional. For each method, there is an analogous method for trying to dispose of would-be necessarily true propositions of the form

(1) q is inductive evidence for p

[1] Blackburn (1973), pp. 26–31; cf. pp. 30–1 above   [2] Lewy (1968) p. 137

If there are necessarily true propositions of form (1) then there are values of G and H, where G and H are related properties of the sort possessed by q and p, when, for example, p is the best explanation of q, such that to be a G-type proposition is *inter alia* to be inductive evidence for an H-type proposition. The analogue of Moore's second method would be to argue that if to be a G-type proposition is *inter alia* to be inductive evidence for an H-type proposition then, absurdly, the proposition

(e) q is inductive evidence for p if q is a G-type proposition and p is an H-type proposition

is identical to the proposition

(f) q is a G-type proposition and p an H-type proposition if q is a G-type proposition and p is an H-type proposition

But so far from being able to show, for *every* natural or metaphysical property F, the falsity of the corresponding proposition 'To be good is to be F', it is not clear to me that Moore's methods will show this for *any* natural or metaphysical value of F. I can bring out my doubts by considering Lewy's defence of one particular application of the second method.

Lewy holds that we can show, by means of the second Moorean method, that to be good is not to be one of the things we desire to desire.[1] Take being F as being something we desire to desire, and consider to begin with the argument that to be good is not to be F because if it were then, absurdly,

(a) To be good is to be one of the things which are F

would be identical to

(b) To be one of the things which are F is to be one of the things which are F

According to Lewy this is a clearly invalid argument. If it were valid, then you could show by an analogous argument that to be a brother is not the same thing as to be a male sibling. If 'to be good is to be F' entails that (a) is identical to (b) then 'to be a brother is to be a male sibling' entails the clearly false proposition that the proposition 'To be a brother is to be a male sibling' is identical to the proposition 'To be a male sibling is to be a male sibling'. But now, keeping to the

[1] ibid. pp. 140–6

same interpretation of *F*, consider the argument that to be good is not to be *F* because if it were then, absurdly,

(c) A thing is good if and only if it is one of the things which are *F*

would be identical to the proposition

(d) A thing is one of the things which are *F* if and only if it is one of the things which are *F*

Lewy thinks that this is a perfectly valid argument. We do not have the difficulty we had with the argument about (a) and (b), because the proposition 'A creature is a brother if and only if it is a male sibling' *is* identical to the proposition 'A creature is a male sibling if and only if it is a male sibling'. Furthermore, it is undeniable that if to be good is to be *F* then (c) is identical to (d), and absolutely clear that (c) is not identical to (d). That (c) is not identical to (d) follows from the fact that it is logically possible to doubt (c) without doubting (d); and each of these things follows from the fact that while (d) is necessary (c) is contingent.

But if it is a necessary condition for two sentences to express one and the same proposition that it is logically impossible to doubt the proposition expressed by one of them without doubting the proposition expressed by the other, then I do not see why there is any more reason to suppose that the proposition 'A creature is a brother if and only if it is a male sibling' is identical to the proposition 'A creature is a male sibling if and only if it is a male sibling' than that (c) is identical to (d). Nor, if this is a necessary condition for propositional identity, do I see why the identity of (c) and (d) should follow from the proposition that to be good is to be *F*.

Furthermore, if you are antecedently doubtful about the falsity of 'to be good is to be *F*', then the argument defended by Lewy is I think likely to be question-begging as addressed to you. Your doubts about the falsity of 'to be good is to be *F*' are likely to make you equally doubtful about either (i) if to be good is to be *F* then (c) is identical with (d), or the grounds which Lewy adduces for (ii) (c) is non-identical with (d). One of the grounds which Lewy adduces for (ii) is that (iii) (c) is contingent while (d) is necessary. But if you are doubtful about the falsity of 'to be good is to be *F*' then this will surely make you equally doubtful about whether (c) is contingent. The other ground which Lewy adduces for (ii) is that (iv) it is logically possible to doubt (c) without doubting (d). And I admit that you might well be doubtful about the falsity of 'to be good is to be F' without thereby being made equally doubtful about (iv). But then, reverting to my previous question, if (iv) really does entail that (c) and (d) are non-identical, why should the proposition that to be good is to be F entail that (c) and (d) *are* identical? According to Blackburn, the idea that applications of Moore's second method beg the question arises from the idea that someone proposing that to be good is to be F *can* say that someone doubting (c) is senselessly doubting (d).

> But from the fact that he can say these things, it does not follow that Moore's argument in any sense begs the question. For identifying these doubts is to most people less plausible than giving the analysis. And to point out an implausible consequence of a position, even if it can be accepted by the strong-minded, is to give a good argument, not a question-begging argument, against that position. And what is more, Moore has things the right way round. For it is sounder to use knowledge of which propositions can be doubted as an indication of which analyses are true than it is to use assertions that some analyses are true to dictate which propositions can be doubted. What we doubt, just as much as what we say, is part of the evidence on which analyses must be based.[1]

My very tentative suggestion is that the argument is likely to seem question-begging to waverers about whether to be good is to be F not because someone proposing that to be good is to be F can implausibly deny that doubting (c) is different from doubting (d), but because the non-identity of these doubts is the only premiss of the argument which, as a waverer about whether to be good is to be F, you will not thereby be made equally doubtful about.

If this is right, and if we accept Lewy's objection to the application of the first Moorean method, then there seems little chance of finding an analogue of either method which can be used to dispose of every candidate necessary proposition of form

> (1) q is inductive evidence for p

(b) *Overriding inductive evidence*

The Humean might now reply that even if he cannot show that there are no necessary propositions of the form

[1] Blackburn (1973) pp. 27–8

(1) q is inductive evidence for p

he can at any rate show something else that will equally well serve his purposes, namely that there are no necessary propositions of the form

(1a) q is overriding inductive evidence for p

where q is overriding evidence for p if it is stronger evidence for p than any true proposition is for *not-p*. His ultimate objective is after all to show that we cannot be inferentially justified in believing any proposition by virtue of having inductive evidence for its truth. And if we are to be inferentially justified in believing a proposition by virtue of having evidence for its truth, then this evidence must be overriding (see p. 134 above). We could therefore just as well have formulated his strategy like this: he assumes that if N is to be inductively justified in believing p, then

(E) N is justified in believing that q is overriding inductive evidence for p

and then argues that (E) cannot be satisfied because (i) no one can be justified in believing a contingent proposition of the form

(1a) q is overriding inductive evidence for p

and (ii) no form (1a) proposition is necessarily true. If the Humean can show that no one can be justified in believing a contingent proposition of the form

(1) q is inductive evidence for p

then he will have shown that the same is true of contingent propositions of the form (1a). And even if he cannot show that no form (1) proposition is necessarily true, he can certainly show that there are no necessarily true propositions of form (1a).

I think this is a mistaken objection. For 'q is overriding inductive evidence for p' to be contingent, it is enough *either* that 'q is inductive evidence for p' is contingent *or* that it is contingent that q is stronger evidence for p than any true proposition is for not-p. So it does *not* follow from the proposition that no one can be justified in believing a contingent proposition of form (1) that no one can be justified in believing a contingent proposition of form (1a). If there really are necessary propositions of form (1), as we are supposing that the Humean might now be inclined to concede, then you can be justified in believing the contingent proposition that q is overriding inductive evidence for p by being justified in believing the necessary proposition that q is inductive evidence for p and the contingent proposition that q is stronger evidence for p than any true proposition is for *not-p*. The inductive sceptic might now reply that when 'q is inductive evidence for p' *is* necessarily true, and q itself is also true, then in fact there always will be a true proposition, which is at least as strong inductive evidence for *not-p* as q is for p. But this is to move over to a non-Humean strategy, whose merits need separate discussion.

Before turning to this, it may perhaps be worth asking whether it is in any case possible to show that there are no necessary propositions of form (1a). The question has an independent interest, in relation to the doctrine of criteria. For on one possible version of that doctrine, q is criterial evidence for p only if it is necessarily true that q is conclusive evidence for p,[1] which seems to imply that q is criterial evidence for p only if it is necessarily true that it is in my sense overriding inductive evidence for p. Without being able to show that there is no such thing as criterial evidence, on these assumptions about its relation to overriding inductive evidence, one can I think at least show that q cannot be criterial evidence for p unless p is necessarily true, which is sufficiently destructive of the notion's most usual philosophical employment.

By the definition of 'overriding evidence' 'q is overriding inductive evidence for p' is incompatible with 'there is a true proposition q_1 which is deductive evidence for *not-p*'. For if q_1 is deductive evidence for *not-p* and q is inductive evidence for p then q_1 is stronger evidence for *not-p* than q is for p. Now, any proposition incompatible with a necessarily true proposition is necessarily false. So if a proposition

(1a) q is overriding inductive evidence for p

is necessarily true, then

(2)   there is a true proposition q_1 which is deductive evidence for *not-p*

is necessarily false. But if q_1, in (2), is contingent, and 'q_1 is deduct-

---

[1] Baker (1974) comes close to this interpretation, holding as he does both that criterial evidence is conclusive evidence and (p. 175) that the statement that a criterial relation holds between two sentences is a priori. Cf. p. 144 above.

ive evidence for *not-p*' is necessarily true, then (2) is not necessarily false. And unless *p* is necessarily true, we can always find a contingent proposition q_1 such that 'q_1 is deductive evidence for *not-p*' is necessarily true, viz. any proposition of the form 'Everything *N* says is true and *N* says that *not-p*'. So no form (1a) proposition is necessarily true, unless *p* is necessarily true.

(3) *A non-Humean inductive scepticism*

Despairing of his ability to show that there are no necessary propositions of the form

(1) *q* is inductive evidence for *p*

the inductive sceptic may now turn to a non-Humean method. Once again, he assumes that *N* is inductively justified in believing *p* only if there is a proposition *q* such that

(E) *N* is justified in believing that *q* is overriding inductive evidence for *p*

But this time he assumes the additional requirement that

(D) *N* is justified in believing *q*

and claims that although (D) and (E) may be separately satisfied, it is at least unlikely that they will be satisfied at the same time. More specifically, he argues that (E) is satisfiable only if there is a true proposition of the form

(1) *q* is inductive evidence for *p*

but that, for any plausible candidate for the status of form (1) truth, either the proposition *q* which it refers to is likely to be false, which will prevent (D) from being satisfied, or, if the proposition *q* which it refers to is true, then it is likely that there is also a true proposition q_1, such that q_1 is as strong inductive evidence for *not-p* as *q* is for *p*, which will make it false that *q* is overriding inductive evidence for *p*, and hence prevent (E) from being satisfied.

There are of course problems about the autonomy of the non-Humean method, reasons for wondering whether it is any more independent of scepticism about radical assurance than inductive scepticism of the Humean kind (see pp. 137–143 above). Do we really want a form of inductive justification which conforms to the regressive principle that N is inductively justified in believing p only if he is justified in believing the proposition which he believes to be inductive evidence for p? If justified belief is identified with radical assurance, then whenever we are inferentially justified in believing p, we are liable to want justified belief in the proposition which we believe to be evidence for p. And there are grounds for thinking that we are liable to want radical assurance. But I am not sure that there are any grounds for thinking that we either want or are liable to want an inductive justification which conforms to the regressive principle just mentioned, other than grounds which depend on the identification of justified belief and radical assurance. There are also problems about the non-Humean sceptic's tacit assumption that you cannot be justified in believing a proposition which is false or probably false. But let us waive these difficulties, and grant the sceptic his tacit assumptions about justification and truth, and see whether he is able even on these assumptions to devalue all true propositions of form (1).

There are certainly some prominent candidates for status of form (1) truth, which the non-Humean method would be able to devalue. It is in effect this method which Goodman applies in his discussion of the relation between propositions of the forms 'All previously observed As are Bs' and 'The next A to be observed will be a B'. Suppose that q is 'all previously observed As have been green', p is 'the next A to be observed will be green', q_1 is 'all previously observed As have been grue', where 'grue' means 'either previously observed and green or not previously observed and blue', and r is 'the next A to be observed will be grue'. Then if q is true, so is q_1. And if any proposition of the form 'All previously observed As are Bs' is inductive evidence for a proposition of the form 'The next A to be observed will be a B', then q_1 is inductive evidence for r, and presumably no less strong inductive evidence for r than q is for p. But r entails *not-p*, so if q is true, q_1 is both true and as strong inductive evidence for *not-p* as q is for p. So if q is true it is not overriding inductive evidence for p.

But of course not all ostensible form (1) truths can be dealt with in this way. It may be that we can find some objective characterisation of disjunctiveness on which 'grue' is an essentially disjunctive predicate while 'green' is not and which would allow us to claim that a proposition of the form 'All past observed As are Bs' is inductive evidence for a proposition of the form 'All As are Bs' if and only if

B is not an essentially disjunctive predicate.[1] And in any case
Goodman's technique cannot be applied to such claims as that *q* is
inductive evidence for *p* when *p* is the simplest explanation of *q*.

Perhaps there is another way of applying the non-Humean
method. The most plausible candidates for true propositions of
form (1) are, we might argue, equivalent either to disjunctions or
conjunctions. Consider, for example, the claim that '*q* is inductive
evidence for *p*' is true when *p* is the simplest explanation of *q*.
'Simplest explanation' has many possible interpretations, including
(a) explanation postulating fewer different kinds of entities, and (b)
mathematically simplest explanation (e.g. explanation whose
equations contain fewer arbitrary numerical parameters, or alge-
braic powers with lower values). So if the original claim is to be at
all plausible, the sceptic might say, we should take it to mean *either*
that '*q* is inductive evidence for *p*' is true when either *p* is the simplest
explanation of *q* in sense (a), or *p* is the simplest explanation of *q* in
sense (b), or ... etc., *or* that '*q* is inductive evidence for *p*' is true
when *p* is the simplest explanation of *q* in sense (a) and sense (b)
and ... etc. Suppose we take the disjunctive interpretation. Whenever *q* is both true and *p* the simplest explanation of *q* in one subset
of the senses (a), (b), ..., we are at least likely to be able to find a
proposition *r*, incompatible with *p*, which is the simplest explanation
of *q* in some other subset of the senses (a), (b), ... So if *q* is true and
likely to be inductive evidence for *p*, then there is a true proposition
(namely *q* itself) which is as strong inductive evidence for *not-p* as
it is for *p*. If on the other hand we take the conjunctive interpretation
according to which *q* is inductive evidence for *p* when *p* is the
simplest explanation of *q* in every one of the senses (a), (b), ..., then
q itself is likely to be false. There is unlikely to be a true proposition
which is in every relevant sense most simply explained by one and
the same explanans.

The argument is obviously defective. Suppose we take the disjunctive interpretation and grant that if *q* is true and *p* the simplest
explanation of *q* in one subset of the senses (a), (b), ..., then there is
a proposition *r*, incompatible with *p*, which is the simplest explanation of *q* in some other subset of the senses (a), (b), ... It follows
that if *q* is inductive evidence for *p*, then *q* is inductive evidence for
not-p. But it does not follow that *q* is as strong inductive evidence
for *not-p* as for *p*.

---

[1] See Swinburne (1973) pp. 115–17

At most, the non-Humean method reminds us that the more incontestably necessary a form (1) proposition is, the less likely it is that we can be justified in believing the proposition q which it refers to. Suppose that q stands for a proposition of the form '(a) at time t_1 two metal bars A and B are both heated up; (b) between t_1 and t_2 A expands by 0.005 per cent; (c) A and B resemble each other in every way which is logically compatible with the negation of "if (a) and (b) then between t_1 and t_2 B expands by 0.005 per cent"'. And suppose that p stands for a proposition of the form 'between t_1 and t_2 B expands by 0.005 per cent'.[1] This gives us what looks like a necessarily true interpretation of 'q is inductive evidence for p'. But how *could* one be justified in believing that the two bars resemble each other in *every* way logically compatible with the negation of that proposition? And yet if q is modified, so as to make it more plausible to suppose it capable of justified acceptance, then a corresponding implausibility creeps into the claim that 'q is inductive evidence for p' is necessarily true. q might for instance be capable of justified acceptance if (c) were replaced by 'A and B resemble each other in every currently ascertainable way, which is logically compatible with the negation of "if (a) and (b) then between t_1 and t_2 B expands by 0.005 per cent"'. But then it would be less plausible to suppose that 'q is inductive evidence for p' is necessarily true. And even if you were lucky enough to stumble across two metal bars which resembled each other in every way compatible with the negation of 'if (a) and (b) . . .', this is not actually the sort of discovery you are often likely to make. There would be rather little that we could be inductively justified in believing, if the only propositions which we could be inductively justified in believing were values of p in necessarily true form (1) propositions in which the relations between q and p were as perfectly tailored as the relations between premisses and conclusions in the metal bars example.

But it is one thing to demonstrate the epistemological inefficacy of the strongest candidates for the status of form (1) *necessity*, another to show that for every *true* proposition of form (1) either q is likely to be false, or there is another true proposition q_1 which is as strong evidence for *not-p* as q is for p.

[1] I owe the example to G. R. Grice

7

Moral Scepticism

The aim of this chapter is to show briefly how some central topics in the epistemology of ethics are related to the position I have developed so far. I do this partly by stressing that if there actually are moral propositions whose truth consists in the existence of states of affairs, then they are as much open to scepticism about radical assurance as propositions of the theoretical kind, and partly by following out the question of whether there is a cogent and disturbing moral scepticism which is independent of these doubts about radical assurance.

To have this independence, the moral sceptic must show that there is some form of justified belief in moral propositions which we are liable to want in vain, whether or not we are liable vainly to want radical assurance of their truth. There are at least three ways in which he might try to establish this conclusion. He might in the first place try to show that the truth of a moral proposition cannot consist in the existence of a state of affairs, whereas moral propositions must be thus 'realistically' conceived if they are to be objects of the sort of justified belief we are liable to want: we cannot have the sort of justified belief in moral propositions which we are liable to want if to think that a moral proposition is true is, for example, 'to concur in an attitude to its subject'.[1] Secondly, the moral sceptic might try to show that, whether or not moral propositions are realistically true or false, there is a true causal or deterministic hypothesis with which an important sub-class of moral propositions is incompatible. And thirdly, he might argue that even if moral realism were entirely unproblematical, we still could not be often enough justified in believing moral propositions, because of the difficulty or impossibility of being inferentially justified in believing them by virtue of having 'factual' or 'naturalistic' evidence for their truth. I think that anti-realism itself guarantees the undisturbing quality of any scepticism it supports, that we have no reason to believe that any

[1] Blackburn (1971) p. 24

action is caused in a way which is incompatible with the agent's liberty of indifference, and that anti-naturalistic scepticism has the same seeming dependence on doubts about radical assurance as the inductive scepticism about theoretical propositions which I discussed in the previous chapter. But there is no space for a full discussion of any of these three theses and I confine myself to a few hesitations about anti-realism and the outlines of some analogies between anti-naturalistic moral scepticism and inductive scepticism of the theoretical kind.

(1) *Anti-realism*

It has been thought that, realistically conceived, moral propositions would be too mysterious to exist. The arguments for their mysteriousness are I think plausible and in no way dependent on doubt about radical assurance. Blinkered-looking though it is, the inference to their non-existence might I suppose also turn out to be defensible. But it is not at all clear that any disturbing moral scepticism follows from their non-existence.

One of the mysteries about realistic moral propositions begins with the thought that necessarily, and however we conceive of moral propositions, the man who sincerely asserts a simple moral proposition wants the action it refers to either to be or have been performed. (By a simple moral proposition I mean one to the effect that some actual or possible action of a particular agent is morally good or obligatory. 'Arthur ought to resign' and 'it was a good thing that Arthur became a doctor' are examples. Non-simple moral propositions cannot be less mysterious than their simple counterparts.) Why is wanting the action done a necessary condition for the sincerity of the assertion, and not just a usual but contingently connected accompaniment? It is because moral judgments are necessarily universalisable, in a sense which makes your assertion of a simple moral proposition universalisable only if you would still want an action like that referred to by the proposition to be done or have been done, even if you believed that this similar action had a relation to your interests which was different from that of the action referred to by the proposition. The point is that it cannot be the case that you would still want an action like it done, unless you do actually want it done. What must you believe about the difference between these relations to your interests? It is not simply that you would still want an action like it done even if you believed that this similar action was against your interests. You may already believe that the action referred to by the simple proposition is against your interests. Or the action referred to by the simple proposition may be of a type which makes it self-contradictory to say that a similar action is against your interests: maybe the proposition was 'My father ought to do that which, of all the actions now open to him, is most in my interests'. But perhaps we can say that N's assertion of the basic moral proposition 'x ought to be done' is universalisable if and only if there is a type of action T such that (i) N believes that x is of type T; (ii) N wants all actions of type T to be done; (iii) both 'an action of type T is in N's interests' and 'an action of type T is against N's interests' are self-consistent; (iv) N would still want all actions of type T to be done, whatever he believed about how x, regarded as a type T action, was related to his own interests. You would be making a universalisable assertion about what your father ought to do if you believed that fathers ought always to put the interests of their children above everything else when relations between them have reached a certain pitch, wanted all fathers to act on this principle and would still want your own father to act on this principle if this were to your own detriment and to the benefit of your sister.

I cannot enter here into a proper defence of this psychological interpretation of universalisability. It would be necessary among other things to compare it with views on which the universalisability of an assertion of a simple moral proposition is defined in terms of the acceptance, by the man making the assertion, of a principle at once exemplified by the simple moral proposition and possessed of certain formal properties. So, for example, adapting a suggestion of Hare's, someone might claim that the assertion of 'x ought to be done' is universalisable if and only if there is a type of action T such that (i) N believes that x is of type T, (ii) N accepts the general principle that actions of type T are obligatory, (iii) this general principle can be formulated without using proper names or personal pronouns.[1] Or you might suggest, more plausibly, and taking over Nagel's conception of an objective reason, that the general principle must be of the form,

$$(p)\,(x)\,(Fx \supset p \text{ ought to do } x)$$

where the property must not contain an occurrence of the variable

[1] Cf. Hare (1954–5) p. 198

p which is bound only by the universal quantification which
governs the entire formula.[1]

Suppose, however, we do grant, on grounds of universalisability,
that, necessarily, when you assert a simple moral proposition, you
want the action it refers to to be or have been performed. The
requirement is utterly mysterious on a 'realistic' conception of moral
propositions. You believe that it was a good thing that Arthur
became a doctor, and in believing this you are not just concurring in
an attitude towards Arthur's action, but believing in the existence of
a moral state of affairs. It follows that it is logically impossible for
you actually to believe in the existence of this moral state of affairs
without wanting another state of affairs to exist, i.e. Arthur's having
become a doctor. But there is something paradoxical in the idea of a
state of affairs which it is logically impossible to believe to exist
without wanting some other state of affairs to exist. And there is no
way, in the present case, of dispelling the paradox. It is not, for
instance, a case in which, since propositions about what you want
are incorrigible for you, it follows logically, from the proposition
that you believe that you want Arthur to have become a doctor,
that you want Arthur to have become a doctor. For you can believe
that something is good without believing what follows from the
proposition that you believe it. So there is something ultimately
mysterious about the proposition that Arthur ought to have become
a doctor. There is the same mystery in all realistically conceived
simple moral propositions: it is logically impossible for you to
believe any of them without wanting the actual or possible actions
they refer to to be or have been performed. And there is no similar
mystery in non-realistically conceived simple moral propositions.
There is no mystery in having to want Arthur to have become a
doctor in order to believe that he ought to have become one, if
believing that he ought to have become one is anyway just concurring in an attitude towards his having become one.

It has also been shown, in the most convincing detail, that if, as
realism says, the truth of a moral proposition consists in the existence of a moral state of affairs which it reports, and if the existence
of this state of affairs is not entailed by the existence of other,
naturalistic facts, then mystery results from the additional and
independently plausible supposition that moral properties are
necessarily supervenient on naturalistic properties.[2] Necessarily, if a

---

[1] Cf. Nagel (1970) pp. 90–4   [2] Blackburn (1971) pp. 105–16

moral property M is supervenient on naturalistic properties $N_1, \ldots,$ N_n then a thing will not become M, or cease to be M, or become more or less M than before, without changing in respect of some member of $N_1, \ldots, N_n$ and hence, by contraposition, a thing remaining the same in respect of all members of $N_1, \ldots, N_n$ will not cease to be M. But why *shouldn't* it be logically possible for a state of affairs to keep all its naturalistic properties and yet cease to be a moral state of affairs if, as we are also supposing, there are no naturalistic facts which entail the existence of moral states of affairs? To dispel the mystery, it would be necessary to show that all moral states of affairs are entailed by the existence of naturalistic facts. If only some are, then there is the additional mystery that some moral propositions are mysterious in this way, others only in a different way or not at all.

But suppose you grant the mysteriousness of realistically conceived moral propositions, and even the inference from their mysteriousness to their non-existence. Is the negation of their existence a scepticism of the menacing kind? Some writers would argue, from first principles, that it cannot be. According to Holland:

> The most serious difficulty for the anti-sceptic arises when he claims that goodness is a fact, and that the presence of it or evil in actions is a fact. For in the case of an agreement that is over a matter of fact in the way that agreement in perceptual judgment is agreement over fact, the judgment might very well go 'Yes, that's a pair of hands all right, but who cares?' So the anti-sceptic will have to say that agreement over the moral is not this although it presupposes it. But the representation of the moral element as a matter of a further, consequential kind (cf. the talk of supervenient qualities) will only allow the question 'Who cares?' to enter in all over again.[1]

What Holland goes on to say at this point, as if he were meeting the difficulty which he has identified, is that 'the anti-sceptic should accept without compunction and indeed with relief the denial that the goodness he cares about is a fact, while distinguishing this sharply from the denial that it is a reality. For the reality of value is not one of fact but of meaning. He will not be able to assert *this*, however, without hearing a sceptical interjection that relies on the equation of meaning with convention.'[2] Although there is nothing

[1] Holland (1967) p. 194   [2] ibid.

which Holland seems willing to say about 'realities of meaning' which would make it easier to understand how it can be a condition for believing that something is a reality that one cares about it, it is he thinks as certain as anything can be that we do nevertheless know moral propositions. 'Iago's wickedness was of a particularly foul kind ... the evil is so strong and undiluted that Shakespearian critics have wondered at it in a way that they don't at lesser villainies. They have disagreed about the terms that should be used to sum it up, but they have never on that account been unsure about its nature as evil; *that* we know as well as we know anything.' Someone who denies that knowledge of moral propositions is possible 'must either stand up and be counted as one who does not know what the rest of us know concerning Iago, or else he must apply Moore's principle against his philosophy. I mean the principle embedded in the statement by Moore that I actually know this is a thumb, and if the proposition "this is a thumb" could be shown to be inconsistent with the Sensum Theory, I should say that the Sensum Theory was *certainly* false.'[1]

But maybe it is possible to answer the question independently of Moore's principle. The answer depends partly on what sense if any can be made of the idea of being justified in having the attitudes, concurrence in which the anti-realist would be inclined to identify with the believing of a moral proposition. Are we to say, with Hume, that 'a passion must be accompany'd with some false judgment, in order to be unreasonable; and even then 'tis not the passion, properly speaking, which is unreasonable, but the judgment'?[2] But the answer also depends on why exactly we are supposed to have wanted justified belief in realistically conceived moral propositions, before we recognised that they are too mysterious to exist. If we wanted and continue to want justified belief in realistically conceived moral propositions for its own sake, then we are disturbed by the denial of their existence. But if it was a matter of thinking that believing a false moral proposition was somehow liable, like believing a false theoretical proposition, to thwart our desires, then in denying that there are realistic moral propositions you are also denying that this thwarting is a possible consequence of believing moral falsehoods (cf. p. 118 above). And if it was a matter merely of thinking that the actual existence of moral states of affairs constrains

[1] Holland (1972) p. 269
[2] Hume *Treatise* p. 416

moral agreement and stabilises practical alliances, why should there not also be psychological factors constraining agreement in attitudes? Even to state these possibilities is I think to cast doubt on the existence of a disturbing anti-realist moral scepticism which is independent of doubts about radical assurance.

(2) *Inferential justification*

The other sceptical argument I want to discuss is that even if moral realism were entirely unproblematical, unmysteriously consistent both with the requirement of wanting, and with the joint requirement of non-entailment and supervenience, we could still not be often enough justified in believing moral propositions, because of the difficulty of being inferentially justified in believing them by virtue of having 'factual' or 'naturalistic' evidence for their truth.

I restrict the discussion this time to what we can call basic moral propositions. These are propositions attributing moral goodness or badness, obligatoriness or impermissibility to the actual or possible action of a particular agent, and the logical equivalents of such propositions. We can count both doing something and refraining from doing something as modes of action, and take it that a proposition to the effect that doing something is bad or impermissible is logically equivalent to a proposition to the effect that refraining from doing it is good or obligatory. We shall also need the notion of a basic naturalistic proposition, i.e. a proposition which attributes a natural property to the actual or possible action of a particular agent, where a natural property is, in the definition of Moore which I have already quoted, 'a property with which it is the business of the natural sciences or of psychology to deal, or which can be completely defined in terms of such'.[1] 'Arthur's acceptance of the nomination will prevent him from finishing his symphony' is an example of a basic naturalistic proposition. 'Arthur ought not to have accepted the nomination' is an example of a basic moral proposition. The aim of the argument is to show that we are prevented from being often enough justified in believing basic moral propositions by difficulties about appealing to basic naturalistic propositions as evidence for their truth.

The sceptic's first move is to dismiss the possibility that we can be

[1] Lewy (1968) p. 137

non-inferentially justified in believing basic moral propositions. They are not self-evident, he begins by inviting you to concede; we cannot metaphorically see their truth, in the way that we can 'see' that no proposition is both true and false. Nor is there a special moral experience, enjoyment of which would allow their acceptance to be non-inferentially justified. The justification for believing a basic moral proposition must therefore be inferential. But, according to the sceptic, you will not be inferentially justified in believing a basic moral proposition unless

(A) there is another proposition which you believe to be over-
     riding evidence for it, and which you are justified in believing

and

(B) you are justified in believing that this other proposition is
     overriding evidence for it.

And these two conditions lead to difficulties. Suppose that there is some particular simple moral proposition which you are inferentially justified in believing. Given the necessity for (A), an infinite regress of justification will be avoidable only if there is some proposition which satisfies each of the following three conditions: (i) it is not a basic moral proposition; (ii) you are justified in believing it; and (iii) you believe either that it is overriding evidence for the initial basic moral proposition which you are inferentially justified in believing, or overriding evidence for a basic moral proposition which you believe to be overriding evidence for the initial basic moral proposition which you are justified in believing, or . . ., and so on. But if a proposition is to satisfy each of these three con-ditions it will have to be a basic naturalistic proposition. And if, as we are assuming, you cannot be non-inferentially justified in believ-ing any basic moral proposition, and will not be inferentially justified in believing any basic moral proposition unless (B) is true, it follows that you will not be justified in believing your initial basic moral proposition unless you are justified in believing a proposition of the form 'q is overriding evidence for p', where q is a basic naturalistic proposition which you are justified in believing, and p a basic moral proposition. The sceptic now has two alternative ways of completing the argument, and they are analogous to the two forms of inductive scepticism about theoretical propositions which I discussed in the previous chapter (see pp. 134–5 above). The first method is to show that no one can be justified in believing a contingent proposition of the form

(1) q is evidence for p

and that no form (1) proposition is necessarily true. The second method is to argue that you cannot be justified in believing both that q and that q is overriding evidence for p because for any true proposition of form (1) either q is likely to be false, or there is another true proposition q_1 which is as strong evidence for *not-p* as q is for p.

If recent discussions of 'is–ought' and 'fact–value' relations have more than an intrinsic interest, then this must I think lie largely in their bearing on the soundness or otherwise of this sceptical argument about the inferentially justified believing of basic moral propositions. But if scepticism about radical assurance is true, the argument about inferential justification is itself less interesting than it initially seems. For scepticism about radical assurance already shows us that we are unable to gain that assurance of the truth of basic moral propositions which we are liable to want. Both basic moral propositions and any basic naturalistic proposition which could be evidence for their truth entail the existence of persons with power to act. And on popular assumptions about self-evidence, propositions of that kind are not ones which we can β-assure ourselves to be true (see p. 45 above). But let us suppose that you are unconvinced by scepticism about radical assurance, and want to know whether the argument about inferential justification is both cogent and autonomous.

The moral sceptic can preserve his autonomy only if he is not obliged to make assumptions about the sort of inferential justification we are liable to want, which he is unable to vindicate without identifying justification and radical assurance. In the previous chapter I suggested that in order to show that there are no contingent propositions of the form 'q is inductive evidence for p' which we can be justified in believing, the inductive sceptic about theoretical propositions needs to interpret justification as assurance and assume general regressive principles about evidential assurance which make him dependent on scepticism about radical assurance. He needs to assume either that you are evidentially assured of a proposition's truth only if you are assured of the truth of another proposition which you believe to be evidence for it, or that you are evidentially assured of a proposition's truth only if you are assured that some other proposition is evidence for it. And it is not clear what grounds he can produce for thinking that we want or are liable to want an assurance which conforms to either of these regressive principles, other than grounds for thinking that we are liable to want radical assurance (see pp. 137–42 above). There are similar problems about the autonomy of the moral sceptic's argument about inferential justification, if he completes his argument in the first of the two ways I earlier distinguished, i.e. claims that no one can be justified in believing a form (1) contingency and that no form (1) propositions are necessarily true. And the difficulty emerges even before he has begun his attempt to show that, where *p* is a basic moral proposition and *q* a basic naturalistic proposition which you are justified in believing, you cannot be justified in believing a proposition of the form

(1) *q* is evidence for *p*

For he assumes, at an even earlier stage than this, that you are inferentially justified in believing a basic moral proposition only if

(A) there is another proposition which you believe to be overriding evidence for it and which you are justified in believing

and

(B) you are justified in believing that this other proposition is overriding evidence for it

There are also difficulties about the actual cogency of the earlier stage, and in particular about the moral sceptic's opening dismissal of non-inferential justification.

But we can afford to waive these difficulties because it is fairly clear that the moral sceptic's argument will in any case collapse for essentially the same reasons as Humean and non-Humean inductive scepticism about theoretical propositions. In my discussion of those doctrines I said I would take '*q* is inductive evidence for *p*' to mean that (i) when a proposition like *q* is true so usually at least is a proposition like *p*; either (ii) it is not the case that when a proposition like not-*q* is true so usually at least is a proposition like *p* or (iia) there is an explanatory connexion between *q* and *p*, and (iii) *q* does not entail *p* (see p. 136 above). The definition is general enough to apply to the case where *q* is a basic naturalistic proposition and *p* a basic moral proposition. So if the moral sceptic is to show that there are no necessarily true propositions of the form

(1) q is evidence for p

when q is basic and naturalistic and p basic and moral, he must show that, with these values of q and p, there are no necessarily true propositions of the form

(1a) q is inductive evidence for p

And if he is to show that for every true proposition of form (1), either q is likely to be false, or there is a true proposition q_1 which is as strong evidence for *not-p* as q is for p, then he must show that this goes also for every true proposition of form (1a).

Since basic moral propositions are on my definition contingent (see p. 116 above), my previous argument about criterial evidence shows that if criterial evidence is necessarily overriding evidence there are no criterial necessities of form (1a) (see pp. 148–51 above). But there is still no way of showing that there are no non-criterial necessities of the requisite form. Moorean methods are as question-begging in the moral case as in the theoretical case (see pp. 144–8 above). Nor, having granted that there may be necessities of form (1a), is the moral sceptic able to devalue their truth by adapting the methods of non-Humean inductive scepticism about theoretical propositions. It may well be that whenever it is overwhelmingly plausible that *necessarily q* is inductive evidence for p, q is unlikely to be true. If q ascribes to an action the conjunction of all those natural properties which anyone would be at all inclined to take as telling in favour of the proposition that it ought to be done, then we may well be inclined to say that necessarily q is inductive evidence for p. But we will also be inclined to doubt the actual truth of q. And yet this still leaves us a long way from the conclusion that for every true proposition of the form 'q is inductive evidence for p' either q is likely to be false, or there is another true proposition q_1 which is as strong evidence for *not-p* as q is for p. No less far, in fact, than reflexion on the epistemological inefficacy of the metal bars example left us from the corresponding conclusion in the theoretical case (see p. 154 above).

The most usual counter to the inferential moral sceptic is not however to show the inadequacy of his arguments about inductive evidential relations between basic naturalistic and basic moral propositions, but rather to assert some species of deductive naturalism, which I take as the generic doctrine that where q and p are naturalistic and moral propositions respectively, there are values of q and p such that it is logically impossible for q to be true and p false. This seems to me an ineffective line of attack, and I will try to show why in the next and final section of the chapter.

(3) *Deductive naturalism*

The inferential moral sceptic had to show either that there are no necessarily true propositions of the form

(1) q is evidence for p

where q is basic and naturalistic and p basic and moral, or that for every true proposition of form (1), either q is likely to be false, or there is a true proposition which is as strong evidence for *not-p* as q is for p. In seeming contrast, the deductive naturalist claims that there are values of q and p, which make them naturalistic and moral propositions respectively, such that it is logically impossible for q to be true and p false.

Now certainly it can be shown that some naturalistic proposition strictly implies some moral proposition if we allow that one of the two propositions may be non-basic. Let n be a basic naturalistic proposition and m a basic moral proposition. Then (n or m) is either (i) a moral proposition, or (ii) a naturalistic proposition. If (i) then the moral proposition (n or m) is strictly implied by the basic naturalistic proposition n. If (ii) then (*not-n* or m) and ((*not-n* or m) and n) are presumably also both naturalistic, and the latter strictly implies the basic moral proposition m.[1] But arguments to a disjunction from one of its disjuncts, and arguments of the form '(*not-q* or p) and q, therefore p' are normally question-begging (see p. 27 above). So even if a relation of strict implication is sufficient for the existence of an evidential relation, in the minimal sense which difficulties about necessity are forcing me to make use of in these two chapters (see p. 136 above), it will still not follow that one can be inferentially justified in believing a moral proposition by adducing a naturalistic proposition as evidence for it. For that seems to require the use of an argument which is not normally question-begging.

[1] Cf. Stegmüller (1973) pp. 51–2

So if deductive naturalism is to be a threat to inferential moral scepticism, we must take it as the thesis that you can actually be inferentially justified in believing a basic moral proposition by virtue of having deductive evidence in the form of a basic naturalistic proposition. The sceptic can now reply that this kind of inferential justification is unlikely to be obtainable when the basic moral proposition is of the form '*S* ought to do *x*'. He can show that every proposition of the form

(2) '*x* is *F*' is deductive evidence for '*S* ought to do *x*'

where *F* is a natural property and '*S* ought to do *x*' a basic moral proposition, is either false or such that '*x* is *F*' is highly unlikely to be true.

Propositions of form (2) are admittedly not the only propositions of the form '*q* is deductive evidence for *p*', in which *q* is basic and naturalistic and *p* basic and moral. There are also propositions of the form '"*x* is *F*" is deductive evidence for "*x* is good"'. But even if the sceptic's thesis applies only to basic moral propositions of the form '*x* is good', the deductive naturalism would still leave an important kind of inferential moral scepticism unscathed.

What then is the argument for our sceptical thesis about propositions of form (2)? Suppose that *F* and *G* are natural properties and that *x* and *y* are incompatible actions each of which it is at one and the same time within the power of some agent *S* to perform, and that it is logically possible that both *x* is *F* and *y* is *G*. Now consider a proposition

(2) '*x* is *F*' is deductive evidence for '*S* ought to do *x*'

and a proposition

(3) '*y* is *G*' is as strong evidence for '*S* ought to do *y*' as '*x* is *F*' is for '*S* ought to do *x*'

The first thing we must note is that (2) will be incompatible with the conjunction

(4) *x* is *F* and *y* is *G* and (3)

For necessarily if (2) is true then (3) is true only if '*y* is *G*' is deductive evidence for '*S* ought to do *y*'. But necessarily if (2) is true then '*y* is *G*' is deductive evidence for '*S* ought to do *y*' only if either '*x* is *F*' or '*y* is *G*' is false. For '*S* ought to do *x*' and '*S* ought to do *y*' are incompatible, and necessarily if *q* entails *p* it is false that *q* is true and that there is a true proposition which entails a proposition incompatible with p.

Next, if (2) is true and incompatible with (4) then (4) is necessarily false. For (2) is necessarily true if true at all, and any proposition incompatible with a necessarily true proposition is necessarily false. But now, a conjunction cannot be necessarily false unless either (i) at least one of its conjuncts is necessarily false or (ii) its conjuncts are so related that they cannot all be true together. But 'x is F' and 'y is G' are each contingent, and for any value of F on which 'x is F' is not highly unlikely to be true, there is a value of G on which (3) is not necessarily false. And if, as we are supposing, 'x is F' is compatible with 'y is G' the three conjuncts do not form an inconsistent triad. So unless 'x is F' is highly unlikely to be true, (2) is false. (The argument will not work if we substitute 'x is good' and 'y is good' for 'S ought to do x' and 'S ought to do y' because even if x and y are incompatible actions which are at one and the same time within the power of S, there is no contradiction in saying that both x and y are good.)

The crucial claim is that for any value of F on which 'x is F' is not highly unlikely to be false, there is a value of G such that

(3) 'y is G' is as strong evidence for 'S ought to do y' as 'x is F' is for 'S ought to do x'

To make this plausible, let us consider some of the particular values of F which have been canvassed by deductive naturalists.

G. R. Grice has claimed that if F is that property of an action which consists in its being in the interests of each person to make a contract with everyone else to perform actions like it, then 'x is F' is a 'ground' of 'S morally ought to do x'. He does not fully explain what a ground actually is, but does at any rate make it clear that q is a ground of p only if q implies p, and furthermore that this latter relation holds if and only if (1) it is logically impossible that q is true and p is false, and (2) the impossibility is not a consequence of either the impossibility of q or the necessity of p.[1] Suppose then that if q is a ground of p then q is deductive evidence for p. It will not be true that

(2) 'x is F' is deductive evidence for 'S ought to do x'

on Grice's interpretation of F, if there is another property G and an action y such that (i) it is logically possible that both x is F and y is G, where x and y are incompatible actions both of which are at one

[1] Grice (1967) pp. 2–3

and the same time within the power of S; and (ii) it is not necessarily false that

(3) 'y is G' is as strong evidence for 'S ought to do y' as 'x is F' is for 'S ought to do x'

Suppose we let G stand for the property of maximising the general happiness. Then it is logically possible both that doing something should have Grice's contractual property and that forbearing from it should have G. But a utilitarian would not say something necessarily false if he said that the proposition that forbearing from something will maximise the general happiness is as strong evidence for the proposition that you ought to forbear from it as the proposition that doing something has Grice's contractual property is for the proposition that you ought to do it. Hence (2) is false, when F stands for Grice's contractual property.

Naturally enough, Grice does himself produce some objections to utilitarianism. He cites cases in which it is logically possible for utilitarianism to yield supposedly absurd conclusions about what ought to be done. It can yield the conclusion that it is wrong to do good to yourself when the only alternative is to do slightly more good to someone else. And it can yield the conclusion that it is completely indifferent whether or not I keep a promise to A, if I can produce as much happiness for B by breaking my promise as I can for A by keeping it.[1] But do such cases show that a utilitarian interpretation of (3) is necessarily false? Cases of this sort may show that it is not necessarily true that

(3) 'y is G' is as strong evidence for 'S ought to do y' as 'x is F' is for 'S ought to do x'

with a utilitarian interpretation of G. But that it is *logically possible* that forbearing from x should both maximise the general happiness and have a property incompatible with its obligatoriness, is perfectly consistent with its being true, of the actual world, that if something is a happiness-maximising forbearance from x then this is as strong evidence for its obligatoriness as the possession of Grice's property is for the obligatoriness of actually doing x. Nor would it help to fall back on the thesis that there are actual as well as logically possible cases in which forbearing from x is at once happiness-maximising and non-obligatory. If there are enough cases

[1] ibid. pp. 57–63

like this, then (3) will be false. But no amount of cases like this will show that (3) is necessarily false.

Or again, Warnock seems in effect to hold that 'x is F' entails 'S ought morally to do x' when 'x is F' means that x manifests one or other of those dispositions which better the human condition by countervailing limited sympathy. He thinks that there are at least four general dispositions of this kind: 'somewhat crudely named, those of non-maleficence, fairness, beneficence, and non-deception'.[1] Should we say then that 'x is F', so interpreted, is deductive evidence for 'S ought to do x'? Suppose that it is fair to do x but beneficent to forbear from x. Warnock himself stresses that this is a logical possibility. It will then be logically possible that an action has Warnock's disjunctive property F and that some incompatible action has the property G of being beneficent. But it does not seem to be necessarily false that the proposition that it is beneficent not to do x is as strong evidence for the proposition that you morally ought not to do x as the proposition that x is F is for the proposition that you ought to do x. So if F, in (2), is taken as Warnock might well want to take it, then we can once more show that the resulting interpretation of (2) is false.

A final example. Richards's system of contractualism, interpreted as a counter to inferential moral scepticism, would entail

(2) 'x is F' is deductive evidence for 'S ought to do x'

when F stands for the property of being enjoined by principles which

> if publicly known and generally acted on, perfectly rational ego-
> istic men . . . from a position of equal liberty, and in the absence
> of any knowledge of their own particular desires, nature and
> circumstances, but with knowledge of all other circumstances of
> human life and desire, would agree to as the standards to be used
> in regulation of their natural relations to one another, whether in
> their common institutions or apart from them.[2]

And this makes it open to much the same objection as the parallel thesis urged by Warnock. For Richards's value of F is also, despite appearances, disjunctive. Richards admits that which principles would be agreed on by egoists in the situation he describes depends

[1] Warnock (1971) p. 86
[2] Richards (1971) p. 80

on the choice they make from among a range of various possible strategies for decision in a state of uncertainty. On the Laplacean strategy, each egoist would assume that the chances of losing or gaining by conforming to any given principle are equal and then decide which principle to agree on by maximising expected value. On the maximin strategy each egoist would consider the worst possible result of conforming to each of a range of principles, and agree to the principle which had the best worst result. Richards accepts that the principles which would be agreed on by egoists who employed the maximin strategy would conflict with those which would be agreed on by egoists who employed the Laplacean strategy. So if his property is to be non-disjunctive, the preferability of one of these strategies must somehow be extracted from the requirement of perfect rationality. He accordingly tries to show that the maximin strategy has a special rational appeal. He points out that

> what is at stake here is not merely an isolated gamble, where a person may indulge his taste for risk-taking, at no great sacrifice to his life on the whole; but the choice of the basic and ultimate standards to which he will be able to appeal in justifying changes in distribution throughout his entire life, where there is no possibility of recouping possible gambling losses later on. Further, since those principles will apply not only to each contractor, but to those he may love and support, the possibility of exercising a gamble, which may be disastrous not only to himself but to those he loves, will further inhibit the propensity to risk-taking.[1]

But it seems to me that these considerations would only have over-riding weight if we made certain assumptions about what the egoist does actually stand to gain or lose by agreeing to one principle rather than another. Richards himself cites the case 'where one has a choice between two acts, a and b, where two circumstances, S_1 and S_2, of whose exclusive probabilities of occurrence one has no knowledge, condition the result of these acts, leading to the following pay-off matrix:

	S_1	S_2
a	0	100
b	1	1'[2]

According to the maximin criterion b must be chosen, since it leads

[1] ibid. pp. 113–14   [2] ibid. p. 113

to the best worst result. But surely this is an irrational choice since the difference between the two worst results is minute, and the difference between the two best results enormous. According to Richards, this sort of case is irrelevant since it is false 'as a matter of sociological and moral fact, that the lowest positions, which different substantive moral principles justify, differ inconsequentially in their utilities, and that the utilities of the highest positions . . . differ substantially'.[1]

It would of course be perfectly possible to find a value of F in

(2) 'x is F' is deductive evidence for 'S ought to do x'

which would make it difficult to find a value of G for which we could claim that

(3) 'y is G' is as strong evidence for 'S ought to do y' as 'x is F' is for 'S ought to do x'

is not necessarily false. All we need do is make 'F' comprehensively conjunctive. Imagine, if you like, that the conjuncts are Grice's property and all the components of Warnock's and Richards's disjunctions. Or, less mechanically, that 'F' in 'x is F' is deductive evidence for 'S ought not to do x' is the typification of the most unmitigatedly mean and brutal piece of hypocrisy you are able to imagine.[2] But the more comprehensive the conjunction, and the more difficult it therefore becomes to find a value of G on which (3) is not necessarily false, the more unlikely it is that 'x is F' is actually true. How often are we in a position to choose whether or not to do something which is simultaneously fair and beneficent and non-deceptive and enjoined by the sort of principle which would be agreed on by ignorant but rational egoists unconstrained in their decision-theoretic preferences and such that it is in the interests of each person to make a contract with everyone else to perform actions like it? Or: 'Iago's wickedness was of a particularly foul kind . . . the evil is so strong and undiluted that Shakespearian critics have wondered at it, in a way that they don't at lesser villainies' (see p. 160 above). The idea that such a thing couldn't happen *really* is, as William Empson remarks somewhere, 'a rather innocent bit of optimism'. How should one describe the idea that it happens often enough to be a paradigm object of moral knowledge?

[1] ibid.
[2] For a comprehensively conjunctive value of F on which 'x is F' is supposed to entail 'x is morally good', see Meynell (1971).

8

On being without radical assurance

In the last two chapters I have been suggesting that scepticism about radical assurance may enjoy a certain primacy in relation to some prominent doubts about justification in ethics and the inductive inference of theoretical propositions. It seemed that, if successful, anti-realistic moral scepticism might guarantee its own innocuousness. And even if the inferential scepticisms, moral and theoretical, were able finally to devalue the existence of necessary evidential relations, and did not depend on the tacit identification of justification and radical assurance, they were not able finally to deny or devalue the existence of all relevant evidential relations. I want now in this final chapter to look once more at our actual desire for radical assurance. The question is whether we can be somehow consoled for our inability to have that radical assurance, or power to gain it, which I earlier argued that we are liable to want.

You could imagine a man bound firmly to begin with in some vast harnessing of the will for the transformation of the world, marching with an army guided at every contingency by an ostensibly consistent series of authoritative directives, its ultimate victory assured by the workings of history or divine grace, its approximate destination discoverable by the unaided power of the human mind. He passes his youth, you might say, in the arms of Tridentine Catholicism, or even as a Marxist of the 'scientific' mould. Then doubt supervenes: suspicions of internal inconsistency, disenchantment with the traditional apologetics. He falls into a melancholy compound of ideological neutrality and hazy confidence in the powers of reason, hoping that philosophy will ultimately present him with a better elaborated and more firmly grounded system of the world – Utopia, map of knowledge, cosmic economy, history of human progress, moral code – possibly even a renovated version of his own original convictions. But also at this stage he begins to reflect more closely on the scope of reason itself, the sources of knowledge, the character of his belief-system as a whole, and comes to recognise the impossibility of gaining the assurance of truth which he now recognises he would like to have. In a word, he accepts the doubts about radical assurance which I have so far been trying to articulate. The question now is: What further development can we expect in his attitudes and opinions? We cannot expect him merely to join Hume in a muffled sigh of relief at the 'whimsical condition of mankind'. Nor is there any reason why he should be impressed by the traditional consolations of stoical ethics or psychology. 'It is perverse,' says Ayer, 'to see tragedy in what could not conceivably be otherwise.'[1] 'Nothing is more certain,' Hume mildly assures us, 'than that despair has almost the same effect upon us as enjoyment, and that we are no sooner acquainted with the impossibility of satisfying any desire, than the desire itself vanishes. When we see that we have arrived at the utmost extent of human reason, we sit down contented.'[2] Our man, by contrast, might find it easier to agree with Swift: 'The stoical scheme of supplying our wants by lopping off our desires is like cutting off our feet, when we want shoes.'

(1) *Wanting and believing*

I claimed in Chapter 3 that a man reflecting about what he wants of his belief-system as a whole is likely to want things of it which he cannot jointly possess unless he is radically assured of the truth of each member of the essential core of that system. Suppose now that the man asks himself *why* he should want a belief-system with these particular features. He may then think either that such a belief-system would be intrinsically valuable, or that its value would lie in its unique contribution to some further intrinsically valuable end. But now questions arise about his assurance that this rationale for wanting radical assurance is actually true. And perhaps there is some chance of consolation, at this point, for the futility of the wanting itself.

Why then *should* you want radical assurance of the truth of each member of the essential core of your belief-system? Consider to begin with the theoretical propositions in the essential core. (i) You could claim merely that there is something intrinsically valuable about each of the features whose conjunction would give you

[1] Ayer (1956) p. 41
[2] Hume *Treatise* p. xxii

radical assurance of the truth of each theoretical proposition. (ii) You could claim that there is an intrinsic value in believing the truth and that if you have radical assurance of the truth of each theoretical proposition, you will believe more of the truth than if this is not the case. (iii) Consider those theoretical propositions which are about means to the ends of your activity. You could claim that if you are radically assured of the truth of each theoretical proposition, more of these practically relevant propositions will be true than would otherwise have been the case, and hence fewer of your wants will remain unsatisfied. (iv) Suppose you have wants whose satisfaction depends on alliances with other people. Maybe such wants are more likely to be satisfied if joint action is based on the fact that you are all radically assured of the truth of the same propositions about the most effective strategy than if it is merely the case that everyone believes the same propositions. Perhaps if people are radically assured of the truth of the propositions they believe in common, their agreement is more stable than it would be if it were the mere outcome of uniform prejudice or a million convergent acts of faith. Having once by his own conscious and deliberate activity non-coincidently grasped the real truth a man may perhaps be less likely to change his mind about its nature than if his belief is the product of habit or guesswork. There would be more scope for making him see reason when he is inclined to change his mind.

Some of these claims about the value of radical assurance could be extended to moral propositions. You could claim that radical assurance about the truth-value of moral propositions is valuable as an end in itself, and likewise that the believing of true moral propositions is an end in itself. You might also claim that practical alliances are more stable when based on radical assurance of the truth of propositions about the moral value of means and ultimate objectives rather than on a mere common believing of these propositions. Maybe the alliance gains power from the possibility that reason and not just physical or psychological force can be brought to bear on people who do not accept its objectives. It is not clear that you could sensibly extend the third claim about theoretical propositions. If I act on a false theoretical proposition then I may be at some stage disappointed. But one can believe that there are true moral propositions, and perhaps even moral propositions whose truth consists in the existence of a state of affairs, without supposing that they correspond to a reality able to touch one's will in the same way as the reality to which true theoretical propositions correspond (see p. 118 above).

Now suppose that you can β-assure yourself of the falsity of each of these claims about the value of radical assurance. Then failing some other rationale for wanting to be radically assured of the truth of each member of the essential core of your belief-system, you would I think be consoled for the futility of wanting it. But of course it is not possible for you to β-assure yourself of the falsity of all these claims about the value of radical assurance on the assumptions about the scope of self-evidence which I initially set out. There is nothing in these assumptions, nor for that matter in the conclusions I reached about moral scepticism in the previous chapter, which prevents you from β-assuring yourself that there is no intrinsic value in radical assurance or that there is no intrinsic value in believing the truth. But each of the claims I considered about the instrumental value of radical assurance relies on a theoretical proposition which you cannot on my initial assumptions about self-evidence β-assure yourself to be false. You cannot, for example, β-assure yourself that such-and-such a condition will or will not stabilise a practical alliance.

So we have to consider a more complex form of consolation. Let us call a set of propositions a π-set if all the members of S are either propositions of the form 'N believes p' or propositions of whose truth my initial assumptions about self-evidence allow you to gain β-assurance. And let us say that a proposition is one of whose truth N can gain γ-assurance if it is entailed by a π-set. I think that being γ-assured of the falsity of one's rationale for wanting more radical assurance than one can get would be almost as much of a consolation as being β-assured of its falsity. You would not after all be happy about believing that scepticism about radical assurance was something to worry about, if you were worried about the fact that you had no radical assurance that you actually believed it.

Now, you can be γ-assured that p if you can be β-assured that p. And we have seen that my initial assumptions about the scope of self-evidence do not prevent you from being β-assured of the falsity of some parts of the rationale for wanting radical assurance, the parts namely which consist in claims about its intrinsic value or the intrinsic value of believing the truth. The question, then, is whether you can be at least γ-assured that the remaining parts of the rationale are false. And the answer is that you can be, if you are lucky enough in what you happen to believe. The remaining parts of the rationale are that without radical assurance there would be less chance of satisfying your wants through individual or collective action. You can actually be γ-assured that such claims are false if you are lucky enough to believe that you already possess everything, other than radical assurance, which you would have wanted if you had not possessed it, or, as we can say, believe a doctrine of providence.

I envisage a two-stage argument. The first stage draws out a feature of doctrines of providence. It is clear I think that a consistent person who always believes a doctrine of providence will not merely never *believe* that he has any unsatisfied wants, other than the desire for radical assurance, but also never actually *have* any unsatisfied wants besides this. This follows because it is a logically necessary condition for wanting something that you believe that you do not possess it and believe that having it would satisfy a want, and because it is inconsistent to believe both of these two propositions and also a doctrine of providence. (Of course it is perfectly consistent to say (leaning back in one's armchair and surveying the porcelain), 'I've got what I want'; but that seems equivalent to: 'I've got the things that satisfy the wants I did have and would still have if I hadn't got those things', and not 'There are things which I've got but nevertheless still want'.)

The ideal conclusion of the second stage of the argument is that a man can be at any time γ-assured that he will from that time onwards believe a doctrine of providence. This conclusion I cannot reach. But I offer the following weaker thesis as a possible substitute: you can be γ-assured that you cannot stop believing a doctrine of providence, as a result of investigations sufficient to make you evidentially assured of its falsity, unless you stop believing a proposition, which is either true or one of whose truth popular assumptions about self-evidence allow you to be β-assured.

Let us say that a set of propositions S is A-coherent for N at time t if each member i of S is such that (i) at t N consciously believes i; and (ii) at t N consciously believes that some other member of S is deductive evidence for i. And let us suppose that

(1) if there are two propositions q and p such that you consciously believe q and consciously believe that q is deductive evidence for p then you cannot stop believing p as a result of investigations sufficient to make you evidentially assured of its falsity

unless you first stop either consciously believing q or consciously believing that q is deductive evidence for p

If (1) is true and N believes at t a set of propositions S which is A-coherent for him at t, then it is not possible that he should at some subsequent time $t + n$ stop believing S, as a result of assuring himself that one or more members of S is false, unless one or other of the following three events takes place after t and before $t + n$: (a) He stops being aware that he believes some member of S which he nevertheless continues to believe; (b) He stops being aware that he believes, of some member of S, that some other member of S is deductive evidence for it, although he does in fact continue to believe this proposition about the evidential relation; (c) He stops believing, even unconsciously, that some other member of S is deductive evidence for this member of S. If either (a) or (b) occurs then N stops believing a true proposition. For to be aware that you believe something is to believe a true proposition to the effect that you believe it. And if (c) occurs, then N will stop believing a proposition of whose truth he can be β-assured. For propositions of the form 'q is deductive evidence for p' are ones of whose truth he can be β-assured. So if (1) is true and N believes at t a set of propositions S which includes a doctrine of providence and is A-coherent for him at t, then it is not possible that he should at some subsequent time $t + n$ stop believing this doctrine of providence as a result of investigations sufficient to make him evidentially assured of its falsity unless he stops believing either a true proposition or a proposition of whose truth he can be β-assured.

Before advancing any further, I will try to consolidate the argument so far. According to (1), it is a necessary condition for you to stop believing p as a result of investigations sufficient to make you evidentially assured of its falsity that *either* you first stop consciously believing any proposition q which you consciously believe and consciously believe to be deductive evidence for p or you first stop consciously believing that this proposition q is deductive evidence for p. Suppose N satisfies the conditions required by (1) for stopping to believe S as a result of the relevant investigations by first stopping consciously to believe some member of S. Is it not possible for him to stop consciously believing it by just stopping to believe it altogether, rather than by continuing to believe it unawares? The answer is that if, after t but before $t + n$, he stopped believing this member of *S* altogether, then he would *ipso facto* stop believing *S*, and therefore could not stop believing *S* at $t + n$. We are interested in those necessary conditions for his stopping to believe *S* at $t + n$ whose satisfaction does not make that event impossible. And either (a) or (b) or (c) must occur after *t* and before $t + n$ if (1) is true and these necessary conditions are to be satisfied. It is true of course that if either (a) or (b) or (c) occurs then *S* stops being *A*-coherent for *N* at the time of its occurrence. But there is no inconsistency between *S*'s ceasing to be *A*-coherent for *N* at a particular time, and *N*'s continuing to believe *S* after that time, and therefore no inconsistency between *S*'s ceasing to be *A*-coherent after *t* but before $t + n$ and *N*'s ceasing to believe *S* at $t + n$. Another way of bringing out the central point of the argument so far is to suppose by contrast that *N* believes at *t* a set of propositions *S* each member *i* of which is such that (i) at *t* *N* consciously believes *i*, and (ii) there is a proposition *k* such that (a) at *t* *N* consciously believes that *k* is deductive evidence for *i* and (b) at *t* *N* consciously believes *k*. Even if (1) is true, it can now perfectly well be the case that at some subsequent time $t + n$ *N* stops believing *S*, as a result of the relevant investigations, even though there is no time after *t* but before $t + n$ at which he has stopped believing a proposition which is either true or one of whose truth he can be β-assured. It is necessary only that, after *t* but before $t + n$, he should have stopped consciously believing one of the *k*-propositions which, at *t*, he believed to be deductive evidence for some member of *S*. If there is some *k*-proposition which he goes on believing unawares then he will stop believing a true proposition. But he can equally well just stop believing some *k*-proposition altogether. If he does the latter then he will not *ipso facto* stop believing *S* itself because the *k*-propositions are not necessarily themselves members of *S*. Equally, he will not *ipso facto* stop believing a proposition which, being of the form '*q* is deductive evidence for *p*', is one which he can β-assure himself to be true. For the *k*-propositions are not necessarily of that form.

Now consider a proposition of the form

(A) *N* believes at *t* a set of propositions which includes a doctrine of providence and which is *A*-coherent for him at *t*

N can γ-assure himself that a proposition is true if it has, as deductive evidence in its favour, a set of propositions each member of which is either of the form '*N* believes *p*' or a proposition of whose truth my initial assumptions about self-evidence allow him to gain β-assurance. So *N* can γ-assure himself of the truth of any proposition of form (A). So also of the truth of any proposition for which a proposition of the form (A) is deductive evidence. And so also of the truth of any proposition for which there is deductive evidence in the shape of the conjunction of a proposition of form (A) and a further proposition of whose truth he can γ-assure himself. Now, *N* can γ-assure himself that

(1) if there are two propositions *q* and *p* such that you consciously believe *q* and consciously believe that *q* is deductive evidence for *p* then you cannot stop believing *p* as a result of investigations sufficient to make you evidentially assured of its falsity unless you first stop either consciously believing *q* or consciously believing that *q* is deductive evidence for *p*

For he can β-assure himself that if you stop believing *p* as a *result* of investigations sufficient to make you evidentially assured of its falsity, then you stop believing *p* after these investigations are completed. And he can β-assure himself that if the investigations are *sufficient* they must involve the affirmation that there is no true proposition *q* which is as strong evidence for *p* as the evidence actually adduced for *not-p* is for *not-p* (see p. 29 above). Accordingly, *N* can γ-assure himself of the truth of the proposition, for which, as we have seen, the conjunction of (1) and a form (A) proposition is deductive evidence, that he cannot stop believing a doctrine of providence as a result of investigations sufficient to make him evidentially assured of its falsity unless he stops believing a proposition which is either true or one which he can β-assure himself is true. The argument is not that anyone sanguine enough to believe certain things about the stability of his belief in a doctrine of providence can be conscious that he does believe these things and hence be γ-assured of their truth. It is that anyone lucky enough to suppose that he does believe certain things which include a doctrine of providence can deduce something about the stability of his beliefs from the mere proposition that he has these beliefs, and hence be γ-assured, not merely that he *believes* that his beliefs have this stability, but that they *do* have this stability. Nor is there anything unduly restrictive in the provisos that you stop believing a doctrine of providence as a *result* of investigations sufficient to make you *evidentially* assured of its falsity. Assurance of the falsity of such a doctrine would presumably be evidential rather than experiential, and based furthermore on investigations which, not being totally conclusive, would allow cessation of belief to occur after their own completion.

You will object that there cannot in fact be a set of propositions which includes a doctrine of providence and every member of which is entailed by some other member, so that if anyone really did believe a set of propositions S which included a doctrine of providence and was A-coherent for him, he would believe something false *about S*. I might fall back on the supposition that the set is infinite. In this case each member of it could be entailed by some other member, even though no two members were logically equivalent. Alternatively, I might put forward a second substitute thesis which turns out to be invulnerable to the objection we are now considering.

The second substitute thesis is that you can γ-assure yourself that, unless you stop believing a proposition which is either true or one which you can β-assure yourself to be true, investigations sufficient for evidential assurance of its falsity cannot stop you believing that, probably at least, you cannot stop believing a doctrine of providence. Let us say that a set of propositions S is B-coherent for N at time t if for each member i of S there is a proposition k such that (i) N consciously believes k; (ii) N consciously believes that k is deductive evidence for 'Probably at least N cannot stop believing i'; (iii) k is a conjunction each conjunct of which is either a member of S or a proposition which he can β-assure himself to be true. It will be clear from my previous argument that if (1) is true, and N believes at t a set of propositions S which is B-coherent for him at t, then evidential assurance of its falsity cannot stop him believing that probably at least he cannot stop believing S unless either he stops being aware of what it is that he does believe, or stops believing a proposition which he can β-assure himself to be true. And it will be clear also that from this point we can reach my second substitute thesis.

Would someone who believed a set of propositions which included a doctrine of providence and was B-coherent for him have to believe something false about that set? Can there actually be a set of propositions which includes a doctrine of providence and each member i of which is such that 'Probably at least N cannot stop believing *i*' is entailed by a conjunction each conjunct of which is either a member of *S* or a proposition which he can β-assure himself to be true? This time I think it may be possible to find a set which meets the necessary requirements even though the number of its members is finite and even though no two of its members are logically equivalent. Here is an example of the sort of thing we need.

(1) a doctrine of providence
(2) Usually, when it seems to *N* that he remembers something he does remember it
(3) A principle of induction licensing the inference of (5) from (2) and (9), (6) from (2) and (10), etc.
(4) If *N* believes a proposition *q* of the form 'it seems to *N* that he remembers *p*' then *N* cannot help believing *q* so long as *q* is true
(5) Probably *N* cannot stop believing (1)
(6) Probably *N* cannot stop believing (2)
(7) Probably *N* cannot stop believing (3)
(8) Probably *N* cannot stop believing (4)
(9) It seems to *N* that he remembers repeatedly trying to stop believing (1) and always failing
(10) It seems to *N* that he remembers repeatedly trying to stop believing (2) and always failing
(11) It seems to *N* that he remembers repeatedly trying to stop believing (3) and always failing
(12) It seems to *N* that he remembers repeatedly trying to stop believing (4) and always failing

Let 'ϕp' mean 'probably at least *N* cannot stop believing *p*'. And let '$\phi(p)$ is adequately entailed' mean '$\phi(p)$ is entailed by a conjunction each member of which is either (a) a member of (1)–(12), or (b) a proposition to the effect that *N* believes some particular proposition, or (c) the proposition "for any pair of propositions, if *N* cannot stop believing one member and consciously believes that this member entails the other member then he cannot stop believing the other member"'. If, for each member *i* of (1)–(12) ϕi is adequately entailed then for each *i* there is a conjunction which entails 'probably *N* cannot stop believing *i*' and each conjunct of which is either a member of (1)–(12) or a proposition which he can β-assure himself to be true.

Obviously $\phi(1)$–$\phi(4)$ are all adequately entailed. $\phi(1)$ is entailed by (5), $\phi(2)$ by (6), $\phi(3)$ by (7) and $\phi(4)$ by (8). Now consider $\phi(9)$–$\phi(12)$. According to (4), if N believes a proposition q of the form 'it seems to N that he remembers p', then N cannot help believing q so long as q is true. So the conjunction of (4) and 'N believes (9)' entails that N cannot stop believing (9) so long as (9) is true. So $\phi(9)$ is entailed by the conjunction of (4), 'N believes (9)' and (9), and is therefore adequately entailed. Since analogous conjunctions entail $\phi(10)$–$\phi(12)$, they too are adequately entailed.

Finally, consider $\phi(5)$–$\phi(8)$. This part of my argument will be easier to set out if I number a few more propositions, as follows

(13) The conjunction of (2), (3) and (9)

(14) For any pair of propositions, if N cannot stop believing one member and consciously believes that this member entails the other member, then he cannot stop believing the other member

(15) N consciously believes that (13) entails 'probably (5)'

$\phi(5)$ is entailed by the conjunction $(\phi(13), (14), (15))$. So if there is a conjunction which adequately entails $(\phi(13), (14), (15))$ then $\phi(5)$ is itself adequately entailed. But if there is a conjunction C which adequately entails $\phi(13)$, then $(C, (14), (15))$ will adequately entail $(\phi(13), (14), (15))$. But each of $\phi(2), \phi(3)$ and $\phi(9)$ is adequately entailed. So there is a conjunction which adequately entails $\phi(13)$. So $\phi(5)$ is adequately entailed. Analogous arguments will show that $\phi(6)$–$\phi(8)$ are adequately entailed.

(2) *Other consolations*

What if you are not lucky enough to have an *A*- or *B*-coherent belief-system which contains a doctrine of providence? Another possible consolation for scepticism about radical assurance would consist in the recognition that the very shortage of radical assurance prevents you from radically assuring yourself of the *truth* of any rationale you can think of for actually wanting to be radically assured of the truth of every member of the essential core of your belief-system. We saw in the previous section that on my initial assumptions about self-evidence, there are some parts of a rationale for wanting radical assurance which we cannot β-assure ourselves to be false. But the parts which we cannot β-assure ourselves to be false turn out also to be parts which we cannot β-assure ourselves to be true. There was the claim that people are more likely to act on false propositions in order to satisfy their wants than would be the case if radical assurance were easier to achieve. On my initial assumptions about the scope of self-evidence, we cannot be β-assured that this correlation between radical assurance and true belief exists. There was a claim about the psychology of stable alliances. The activity which culminates in radical assurance would be a stronger cement than anything else which might make for agreement in belief. Clearly that is also not the sort of thing which we can β-assure ourselves to be true, on my initial assumptions about the scope of self-evidence.

There is a wider application, too, for the arguments I developed at the end of the previous section. They show that anyone with an A- or B-coherent belief-system can be γ-assured that it has a certain stability. This conclusion has a special interest to those whose A- or B-coherent belief-systems contain doctrines of providence, because of the special relation between wanting something and believing that you do not possess it. But even if you do not believe a doctrine of providence, you may still for instance be consoled by the thought that there are other propositions which investigations sufficient for evidential assurance of their falsity cannot stop you believing unless first of all you have either stopped being aware of what it is that you do believe or stopped believing something which you can be β-assured is true.

The only other possibility is to make what you can of the fact that it is only epistemological propositions which scepticism about radical assurance need prevent you from believing. You do not become less certain that you have two hands, on reflecting that you would like a belief-system in which, impossibly, that and every other non-adiaphorous proposition you believe is one of whose truth you are radically assured. You need not even become disenchanted with pre-sceptical projects of a purely philosophical kind. You could for example still continue to believe that the division of science from pseudo-science is a division of possible truth from probable falsehood, even if you do not believe that we can have that assurance of scientific truth which we are liable to want in circumstances of philosophical reflexion. You can also continue to accept the optimistic doctrine that there are psychological factors liable to constrain us to believe the truth, that the description of these factors is an aid to their mobilisation and that the philosopher would partially describe them in successfully demarcating science from pseudo-science and in accurately reporting how scientific theories are supposed to be confirmed. It may be worth looking a little more closely at this example, and at a partly parallel example about the demarcation of moral judgments.

Scepticism about radical assurance allows you to go on believing that there are experiences which make certain propositions either psychologically impossible to believe or psychologically impossible not to believe, and that these impossibilities are respectively signs of falsity and truth, and that there is a potential and falsity-indicating psychological impossibility in believing a proposition which is logically incompatible with a proposition which experience makes it impossible to believe. Suppose that a theory is scientific only if it is logically incompatible with some proposition which asserts the occurrence of sensory experience. Scepticism about radical assurance does not prevent you from believing that you are constrained to believe these experiential propositions by the very experience which makes them true, and liable to be constrained to reject the hypothesis which these experiential propositions falsify. The point remains valid if we advance from 'naive falsificationism' to a more refined demarcation-criterion. Let p be a proposition, basic in the Popperian sense (see p. 111 above) and describing the masses, positions and velocities of a certain finite set S of celestial bodies at a certain time, and q a basic proposition describing the position of one of these bodies at a later time. If N is the Newtonian theory of gravitation and dynamics then if (if N then (if p then q)) then r, where r is a proposition to the effect that, between the times referred to by p and q, the movements of the bodies in S are not affected by the movements of other bodies, or by non-gravitational forces. Accordingly, if p is at a certain time conventionally acceptable, but q not, convention and consistency can be just as well served by the rejection of r as by the rejection of N. And there is also the possibility of preserving both r and N and rejecting either the conventions which make p acceptable, or the conventions which make q not acceptable; maybe there is something wrong with the theory of radio-optics presupposed in the construction of the telescopes used to follow the movements of the bodies that p and q refer to; maybe there is some body, not in S, which, although it does not affect the movements of the bodies which p and q refer to, nevertheless prevents us from following its movements properly; and so on. Suppose we generalise from this case. We can have '*T*-proposition' as the label for a proposition like *r*, which has to be true if a theory is to entail a conditional, like 'if *p* then *q*', whose components are basic propositions; and '*O*-proposition' can be the label for a proposition, such as a theory of radio-optics, which is presupposed in the conventional acceptance of a basic proposition. A rather stringent rule would endorse a theory *H* if and only if it belongs to that set of propositions, including a *T*-proposition and some conventionally accepted basic propositions, which provides the simplest known explanation of some set of conventionally accepted basic propositions, and if there are no conventionally accepted basic propositions whose conjunction with *H* and this *T*-proposition entails any conventionally rejected basic propositions. Lakatos proposed a milder rule, which would allow a theory to be endorsed even if it failed the second part of this test: *H* is endorsed if and only if (1) it belongs to that set of propositions S_1 including a *T*-proposition *p* and some conventionally accepted basic propositions, which provides the simplest known explanation of some set of conventionally accepted basic propositions *X*; (2) either (a) there are no conventionally accepted basic propositions whose conjunction with *p* and *H* entails conventionally rejected basic propositions or (b) (i) the conjunction S_2 of *p*, *H* and some conventionally accepted basic propositions entails a set of conventionally rejected basic propositions *Y*, (ii) there is no set of propositions S_3 which explains why S_2 entails *Y*, explains *X*, and entails a set of basic propositions *Z* some of which are conventionally accepted and none of which are entailed by $S_1.S_3$ might contain a more general theory in place of *H*, or a different *T*-proposition in place of *p*, or it might contain *O*-propositions incompatible with those presupposed in the rejection of *Y*.[1] Suppose that a theory is scientific only if, given current conventions and the Lakatos rule, endorsement and non-endorsement are both logically possible. The sceptic about radical assurance can continue to believe that non-endorsement is a sign of both falsity and potentially unavoidable rejection, and interest himself precisely for this reason in the difficult task of applying this more complex demarcation criterion to popular belief-systems all too easily branded as pseudo-scientific by the 'naive falsificationist'.

In the same way, scepticism about radical assurance need not prevent you from continuing to believe that there is truth-indicative

[1] See Lakatos (1970)

agreement or potential agreement in the acceptance of moral propositions. In the case of simple moral propositions consensus is made possible partly by the connexion between believing such a proposition and wanting an action to be done. If I do not want the action done, which a simple moral proposition refers to, I cannot believe that proposition. Nor can I believe it unless I would still want actions like it to be done even if I held beliefs incompatible with those I now hold about how such actions relate to my own interests (see pp. 156–7 above). The sceptic can continue to believe that practical agreement is helped by the existence of more or less obvious psychological limits to what one can want done even when one's own interests are unaffected, and also by the inability of many people to go on wanting things to be done when this would mean that their own interests would suffer as a result. The belief would not be that because a judgment can properly be called moral only if it is in this sense universalisable, there are psychological limits to what can properly be called moral disagreement. It is more that there are psychological pressures to make what can properly be called moral judgments, to see oneself as just one person among others when it comes to deciding what is to be done, and at the same time to see others as one would then have to see oneself. Scepticism about radical assurance need not prevent you from believing that it is a truth-indicative agreement which these pressures are liable to produce.

Works cited

ABBREVIATIONS

AJP   *Australasian Journal of Philosophy*
APQ   *American Philosophical Quarterly*
JP   *Journal of Philosophy*
M   *Mind*
N   *Nous*
PAS   *Proceedings of the Aristotelian Society*
PASS   *Proceedings of the Aristotelian Society Supplementary Volume*
P   *Philosophy*
PQ   *Philosophical Quarterly*
PS   *Philosophical Studies*
R   *Ratio*
RS   *Religious Studies*

P. Achinstein, 'Concepts of Evidence' *M 87* (1978) 22–45
H. Albert, *Traktat über kritische Vernunft* (Tübingen 1969)
W. P. Alston, 'Two Types of Foundationalism' *JP 73* (1976a) 165–85
    'Has Foundationalism been refuted?' *PS 29* (1976b) 287–305
D. M. Armstrong, *Belief, Truth and Knowledge* (Cambridge 1973)
J. L. Austin, *Sense and Sensibilia* (Oxford 1962)
A. J. Ayer, *Language, Truth and Logic* (2nd edn, London 1946)
    The Central Problems of Philosophy (London 1973)
    The Problem of Knowledge (London 1956)
    The Concept of a Person (London 1963)
    Metaphysics and Common Sense (London 1969)
G. Baker, 'Criteria: A New Foundation for Semantics' *R 16* (1974) 156–89
W. Bartley, *The Retreat to Commitment* (London 1964)
S. Blackburn, 'Moral Realism' in J. Casey (ed.) *Morality and Moral Reasoning*
    (London 1971)
    Reason and Prediction (Cambridge 1973)
    'The Identity of Propositions' in S. Blackburn (ed.) *Meaning, Reference and*
    Necessity (Cambridge 1975)
L. Bonjour, 'The Coherence Theory of Empirical Knowledge' *PS 30* (1976)
    281–312
    'Can Empirical Knowledge have a Foundation?' *APQ 15* (1978) 1–14
R. B. Braithwaite, *Scientific Explanation* (Cambridge 1953)
R. Chisholm, *Theory of Knowledge* (2nd edn, Englewood Cliffs 1977)

L. J. Cohen, 'Why should the Science of Nature be Empirical?' in G. Vesey
(ed.) *Impressions of Empiricism* (London 1976) pp. 168–83.
The Probable and the Provable (Oxford 1977)
J. W. Cornman ,'Foundational versus Nonfoundational Theories of Empirical
Justification' *APQ 14* (1977) 287–97
M. Deutscher, 'Reasons, Regresses and Grounds' *AJP 51* (1973) 1–16
R. Edgley, *Reason in Theory and Practice* (London 1969)
R. Fogelin, *Wittgenstein* (London 1976)
K. Gödel, 'What is Cantor's Continuum Problem?' in P. Benacceraf and
H. Putnam (eds.) *Philosophy of Mathematics* (Oxford 1964) 258–73
G. R. Grice, *The Grounds of Moral Judgement* (Cambridge 1967)
A. Grünbaum, *Modern Science and Zeno's Paradoxes* (London 1968)
I. Hacking, 'The Logic of Pascal's Wager' *APQ 9* (1972) 186–92
C. L. Hamblin, *Fallacies* (London 1970)
R. M. Hare, 'Universalizability' *PAS 55* (1954–5) 295–312
G. Harman, *Thought* (Princeton 1973)
R. F. Holland, 'Moral Scepticism' *PSS 41* (1967) 185–98
'Morality and Moral Reasoning' *P 47* (1972) 264–75
Hume, *Treatise of Human Nature* (Selby-Bigge ed.) (Oxford 1888)
R. Jaeger, 'Implication and Evidence' *JP 52* (1975) 475–85
A. Kenny, 'Criterion' in P. Edwards (ed.) *Encyclopaedia of Philosophy*, 2 (New
York 1967) 258–61
Wittgenstein (London 1973)
I. Lakatos, 'Infinite Regress and the Foundations of Mathematics' *PASS 36*
(1962) 155–84
'Falsification and the Methodology of Scientific Research Programmes' in I.
Lakatos and A. Musgrave (eds.) *Criticism and the Growth of Knowledge*
(Cambridge 1970) 91–195
'Popper on Demarcation and Induction' in P. Schlipp (ed.) *The Philosophy
of Karl Popper* (La Salle Ill. 1974) 241–73
K. Lehrer, *Knowledge* (Oxford 1974)
I. Levi, *Gambling with Truth* (New York 1954)
C. Lewy, 'G. E. Moore and the Naturalistic Fallacy' in P. F. Strawson (ed.)
Studies in the Philosophy of Thought and Action (London 1968) 134–46
R. Luce and H. Raiffa, *Games and Decisions* (New York 1957)
J. L. Mackie, *Truth, Probability and Paradox* (Oxford 1973)
The Cement of the Universe (Oxford 1974)
Problems from Locke (Oxford 1976)
A. M. McIver, 'Knowledge' *PASS 32* (1958) 1–24
H. Meynell, 'The Objectivity of Value Judgements' *PQ* (1971) 118–31
T. Nagel, *The Possibility of Altruism* (Oxford 1970)
Pascal, *Pensées* (Pléiade ed.)
Mark Pastin, 'Critical Review of K. Lehrer's *Knowledge*' *N 11* (1977) 431–7
C. S. Peirce, 'Questions concerning certain faculties claimed for man' in
Philosophical Papers 2, (Hartshorne and Weiss eds.) (Cambridge Mass.
1960)
A. Plantinga, *God and other Minds* (New York 1967)
J. Pollock, *Knowledge and Justification* (Princeton 1974)

K. R. Popper, *The Logic of Scientific Discovery* (London 1959)
  Conjectures and Refutations (London 1963)
  Objective Knowledge (London 1972)
A. Quinton, *The Nature of Things* (London 1973)
N. Rescher, *The Coherence Theory of Truth* (Oxford 1973)
D. Richards, *A Theory of Reasons for Actions* (Oxford 1971)
B. Skyrms, *Choice and Chance* (2nd edn, Belmont Calif. 1975)
W. Stegmüller, *Personelle und Statistische Wahrscheinlichkeit (Probleme und Resultate der Wissenschaftstheorie und Analytischen Philosophie Bd. IV*, Erster Halbband) (Berlin – Heidelberg – New York 1973)
P. F. Strawson, *Individuals* (London 1959)
  The Bounds of Sense (London 1966)
R. G. Swinburne, 'The Christian Wager' *RS 4* (1968) 217–28
  An Introduction to Confirmation Theory (London 1973)
G. J. Warnock, *The Object of Morality* (London 1971)
D. Wiggins, 'Freedom, Knowledge, Belief and Causality' in G. N. A. Vesey (ed.) *Knowledge and Necessity* (London 1970) 132–54
B. Williams, *Descartes* (Harmondsworth 1978)
  'Deciding to Believe' in *Problems of the Self* (Cambridge 1973) 136–51
L. Wittgenstein, *Philosophical Investigations* (Oxford 1958)
  On Certainty (Oxford 1969)

Index

9/84
15/84
15/84
17|8
171.
R. A.